W9-AZC-908

C I T Y P A C K
Vienna

By Louis James

2ND EDITION

Fodor's Travel Publications
New York • Toronto • London • Sydney • Auckland

WWW.FODORS.COM

Contents

About this book

Citypack Vienna is divided into six sections to cover the six most important aspects of your visit to Vienna. It includes:

- The city and its people
- Itineraries, walks, and excursions
- The top 25 sights to visit
- What makes the city special
- Restaurants, hotels, stores, and nightlife
- Practical information

In addition, text boxes provide fascinating extra facts and snippets, highlights of places to visit, and invaluable practical advice.

CROSS-REFERENCES

To help you make the most of your visit, cross-references, indicated by ➤, show you where to find additional information about a place or subject.

MAPS

The fold-out map in the wallet at the back of the book is a comprehensive street plan of Vienna. All the map references given in the book refer to this map. For example, the Burgtheater, on Dr-Karl-Lueger-Ring, has the following information: ✚ 66—indicating the grid square of the map in which the Burgtheater will be found.

The city-center maps found on the inside front and back covers of the book itself are for quick reference. They show the top 25 sights, described on pages 24–48, which are clearly plotted by number (**1** – **25**, not page number) from west to east.

ADMISSION CHARGES

An indication of the admission charge (for all attractions) is given by categorizing the standard adult rate as follows:

✋ expensive (over AS100; 7 euros), moderate (AS50–100; 3.5–7 euros), inexpensive (under AS50; 3.5 euros).

VIENNA
life

Introducing Vienna

Vienna's world of art

Over the last decade Vienna's major galleries and museums have been undergoing a hugely expensive program of modernization. In this century's most exciting development, a gigantic new "museum quarter" (► 55), complete with state-of-the-art exhibition halls, has been built on the site of the former imperial stables and provides a new and more appropriate home for the Museum of Modern Art, a special gallery to show the unique Leopold collection of Klimt and Schiele masterworks, a library, and a pioneering "museum of the history of ideas."

Until the 1980s, the city of Mozart, Beethoven, Brahms, and Strauss seemed an aging community. Its trams were full of pensioners glaring at exuberant youth (such as there were); its concert halls and theaters were patronized by a middle-aged and self-satisfied middle class.

The political scene had been enlivened between 1970 and 1983 by a Socialist government led by the charismatic Bruno Kreisky but, although he improved foreign policy, his lax rule entrenched some of the worst aspects of the domestic political culture.

More recently, Austria was ostracized worldwide after the rightest Freedeom Party, formerly led by Jörg Haider, entered into a coalition government with the Conservative People's Party; Haider had made statements that seemed to whitewash Nazi guilt. However, a European Union report cleared the country of anti-democratic behavior, while expressing continuing reservations about certain aspects of the Freedom Party.

Vienna today is a vibrant, modern, and extremely well-run metropolis, energized by an emergent youth culture and by political and social change as well as by the city's longtime

View of the old town

cosmopolitan outlook: Always a magnet for foreigners, the city draws both well-heeled international bureaucrats working in UN agencies and Slavs toiling as *Gastarbeiter* (guest workers) in the construction industry— immigrants number around 16 percent of the population.

Since 1989, Vienna has been vigorously exploiting economic opportunities to the East. At the same time, with Austria's January 1995 entry into the European Union, the city finally found its place among Western European cities political- cal and economic cultures, to which it had theoretically always belonged.

Visitors today will appreciate the considerable energy that has been expended on creating new attractions—notably the Lipizzaner Museum in the Stallburg and the significant Museum Quarter. The revitalized museums now have excellent new bookstores and better cafés. Public transportation, which has always been excellent in Vienna, continues to be further developed. And nowadays, Vienna is looking to the future not only as the business hub of Central Europe but also as a firm tourist favorite, a city where sophisticated modernity coexists with unalloyed nostalgia and a strongly local vernacular culture that's unique on the Continent.

The Haas-Haus on Stephansplatz

Viennese character

The Viennese are great patriots. Dozens of songs with titles like *Vienna, City Of My Dreams*, and *Vienna Will Always Be Vienna* are still sung in local wine taverns; a sub-culture of humor, literature, and song in Viennese dialect continues to flourish. On the other hand, Vienna has been a melton pot since the 19th century, when people from all over the Habsburg Empire moved here: it was said at the time that no family in the city could trace its Viennese antecendents further back than two generations. A generation on, and many of these families will also be "Viennese," a concept that manages to combine narrow provincialism with cosmopolitan assimilation.

VIENNA IN FACTS & FIGURES

About Vienna
- Federal state of Austria, and its capital.

City Symbols
- The Steffl (south tower of St. Stephen's Cathedral, ➤ 43) and the Riesenrad (the giant Ferris wheel on the Prater, ➤ 56).
- Patron saint: Klemens Maria Hofbauer (1751–1820).
- Vienna's coat of arms is a white fesse cross on a red background, a symbol derived from a motif on 13th-century coins.

Surface Area
- In 1857 the order was given to raise the old city's bastions, and thereafter the inner and outer suburbs (1892) were incorporated. Vienna now has 23 districts and a surface area of 160sq miles.

Population
- Since the 1980s, the population has risen for the first time since the end of the Austro-Hungarian Empire in 1919. It now stands at 1.61 million.
- Of the 185,000 Jewish-Viennese who lived here before World War II, 50,000 died in the Holocaust.
- The non-Austrian population stands at more than 16 percent, excluding an estimated 60,000 illegal residents.

Work
- The average Austrian employee was on strike in 1982–1988 for 65 seconds, compared with 55.65 minutes for Americans in the same period; strikes are still almost nonexistent.
- 5,000 people live or work in the Hofburg alone.

Music
- Haydn's marvelous *Kaiserhymne* was abandoned as the imperial anthem after the Germans appropriated it.
- The current Austrian national anthem (Land of Mountains, Land of Rivers) is doubtfully attributed to Mozart.

Location
- The city lies on the River Danube at the foot of Vienna Woods (Wienerwald), on the northern edge of the Vienna Basin at 16°22' longitude east and 48°13' latitude north.

CONTEMPORARY VIENNESE

MARCEL PRAWY

Octogenarian Frydmann Ritter von Prawy combines aristocratic charm and boyish enthusiasm in his mission to spread the gospel of opera to the Austrian public. His long career—as a professor, author, dramatic adviser to the Volksoper and the Staatsoper, and above all as a brilliant TV commentator on opera and operetta—was honored in 1998 with an Austrian "Romy" award. Prawy is a well-known figure around Vienna, riding his bicycle through the city streets. He was made an Honorary Citizen of Vienna in 1992.

ANDRÉ HELLER

Vienna-born Heller never completed his education and began his career as a disc jockey. Since the 1970s he has repeatedly made waves and fomented controversy as a satirist, writer, and the stager of ambitious multimedia shows. Among the most successful of these spectaculars have been the *Teatro del Fuego* (1983) in Lisbon and the traditional Roncalli Circus, which he co-founded in Austria in 1976.

PETER PILZ

One of the most incisive political minds in Vienna is the maverick Parliamentary Deputy, Peter Pilz of the Green Party. He has played a key role in uncovering scandals such as an earlier government's illegal arms trade; he investigated the politically inspired misuse of police data banks revealed by a former member of the Freedom Party, which responded by trying to smear him. Despite his tiny political base, Pilz is a permanent thorn in the side of Austria's often corrupt establishment.

NIKOLAUS HARNONCOURT

Descended from a liberal Habsburg archduke who married a Styrian postmistress, the cellist Nikolaus Harnoncourt is a musical innovator and one of nature's free spirits. Known as "the Karajan of early music" (referring to the famous conductor), Harnoncourt has pioneered authentic performances of classical music in Austria, and is in demand by opera houses all over the world.

Niki Lauda

The most famous Austrian apart from Arnold Schwarzenegger, Lauda won his first motor race in 1968 (a hill climb). After capturing the world championship in 1975 he was almost killed at the Nürburgring in 1976, but made a historic comeback to become World Champion again in 1977 and 1984. He won the Grand Prix 25 times. In 1979 he founded Lauda Air, a successful challenger to the Austrian Airlines monopoly until it ran into trouble in 2000.

Niki Lauda

A CHRONOLOGY

5th–1st century BC	The Celtic Boier tribe settle on the site of what is now the Belvedere Palace.
15 BC	The Romans conquer the area.
AD 400–791	The Romans withdraw. Charlemagne creates the *Ostmark* (Eastern Region of his empire).
881	The Salzburg annals recall a battle *ad Weniam*— the first reference to the name *Wien* (Vienna).
1156	Under the Babenbergs, Austria becomes a dukedom and Vienna the ducal residence.
1278	640 years of Habsburg rule begin.
1421	Pogrom (*Wiener Geserah)* against the Viennese Jews. Two hundred are burned alive, the rest dispatched to Buda in Hungary.
1498	Maximilian I founds the Kapellenknaben, forerunner of the Vienna Boys' Choir.
1517	Advent of Lutheranism in Vienna.
1521	The Spanish and German realms of the Habsburgs, all ruled by Charles V, are divided. Charles's brother, Ferdinand I, takes the Austrian possessions, inheriting Bohemia and Hungary five years later.
1529	First Turkish siege of Vienna.
1551	Ferdinand invites the Jesuits to Vienna. The Counter-Reformation begins.
1683	Second and final unsuccessful Turkish siege.
1781	Joseph II's Edict of Tolerance allows the free practice of religion.
1782	Wolfgang Amadeus Mozart's opera *The Abduction from the Seraglio* premières on July 16 at the Court Theater.
1792	Ludwig van Beethoven settles in Vienna.

1805–1821	Napoleon's troops occupy Vienna in 1805 and 1809. After his defeat, the Congress of Vienna (1814–1815) imposes order on Europe.
1828	In June, Franz Schubert completes *Die Winterreise* song cycle. He dies November 19, age 31.
1848	Revolutions against Habsburg absolutist rule. 18-year-old Franz Joseph becomes emperor.
1857	Franz Joseph decrees the removal of the old city's fortifications and the building of the Ringstrasse (▶ 12).
1867	Formation of the Austro-Hungarian Empire. On February 15 Johann Strauss Junior's *On the Beautiful Blue Danube* is first performed by the Vienna Male Choral Society; it flops.
1897	Vienna Secession founded (▶ 34). On October 12 Gustav Mahler becomes director of the Vienna opera, initiating a "golden age" of imaginative productions.
1916	Franz Joseph dies. The Habsburg Empire is dissolved in 1919.
1922	Vienna becomes one of the Federal States of the Republic of Austria.
1934	Civil War breaks out between the Christian conservatives and the Socialists. Clerico-Fascist dictatorship under Engelbert Dollfuss.
1938	Hitler invades Austria on March 12. This is the *Anschluss* (▶ 12).
1945–1955	Vienna is under joint allied control until the State Treaty restores a free Austrian state.
1979	UNO-City (Vienna International Center) opens.
1995	Austria joins the European Union.
2000	Far right Freedom Party joins government coalition amid international controversy.

People & Events from History

MOZART (1756–1791)
Wolfgang Amadeus Mozart settled in Vienna in 1781. Until his death here, during a period of unparalleled creativity, he composed many of his operas (including *The Magic Flute* and *The Marriage of Figaro*), as well as 21 concertos, over 20 symphonies, 24 string quartets, and 17 masses.

The Austrian Parliament

THE STRAUSS DYNASTY
Johann Strauss the Elder (1804–1849) started the first dance craze of modern times—the waltz—in early 19th-century Vienna. Johann Strauss Junior (1825–1899) later composed some of the most famous waltzes, including *The Blue Danube*. Strauss Junior was deluged with fan-mail and requests for locks of his hair; this Strauss cult foreshadowed the hysteria inspired by today's pop idols.

THE RINGSTRASSE
On Christmas Day 1857 the Emperor Franz Joseph ordered the demolition of the city bastions and the creation of a great boulevard around the city. The Ringstrasse symbolized an era of wealth, industry, modernization, and liberal power in the City Council.

THE *ANSCHLUSS* (1938)
After the *Anschluss*—the annexation of Austria with Germany by Adolf Hitler—many Viennese went into exile, and artistic and academic talent was lost through Austrian-born Adolf Eichmann's successful campaign to make Vienna *judenrein* (Jew-free).

Vienna, city of music
Music has reverberated within the walls of Vienna since the days when the *Minnesänger* (poets of chivalry) performed at the Babenberg court in the 13th century. Some of the Habsburg emperors were themselves composers, and members of the dynasty were patrons of Gluck, Haydn, Mozart, and Beethoven, among many others. Schubert, Brahms, Strauss (father and son), Bruckner, Mahler, and Schönberg are the best known of the many composers who have lived and worked in the city over the past 200 years.

VIENNA
how to organize your time

ITINERARIES

Vienna's old quarter is known as *die Innere Stadt*, and many important sights are here. Walk if possible. Hopper buses (1A, 2A, 3A; ➤ 91) run through the center, as do U-Bahn lines U1 and U3, both of which have a stop at Stephansplatz. Alternatively, take tram 1 (clockwise) or tram 2 (counterclockwise) around the Ringstrasse.

ITINERARY ONE	THE RINGSTRASSE
Morning	Take tram 1 to Burgring from U-Bahn Oper Museum of Art History (➤ 32). Cross the Ring to Burggarten (➤ 56), then recross it southward to reach the Secession Building (➤ 34).
Lunch	Café Museum (➤ 59) for a light lunch.
Afternoon	Cross the Wienzeile to Resselpark and Karlsplatz for St. Charles's Church (➤ 44) and the Viennese History Museum (➤ 45). Cross Lothringerstrasse to the Künstlerhaus and the Concert Hall of the Friends of Music (Musikverein, ➤ 81). Head northeast, past the Imperial Hotel (➤ 84), then walk along the Schubertring to the Stadtpark (➤ 56).

ITINERARY TWO	ANCIENT CENTERS OF HISTORY
Morning	Take U3, or hopper 2A or 3A, to Herrengasse. After coffee in Café Griensteidl ✉ Michaelerplatz 2, spend the morning at the Hofburg (➤ 35): tour the Imperial Apartments (Kaiserliche Appartements) and the Burgkapelle, and watch the Lipizzaner horses (➤ 36).
Lunch	Lunch at Bei Max (➤ 63) for Carinthian and Viennese specialties.
Afternoon	Visit the Schottenstift Museum and Schottenkirche (➤ 38), then walk through Freyung (➤ 38) and Heidenschuss to Am Hof and the Church of the Nine Choirs of Angels (Kirche am Hof). In Schulhof is the Clock Museum (➤ 39). Continue north, via Judenplatz and Wipplingerstrasse, to the Old City Hall (➤ 41).

ITINERARY THREE	VIENNESE ARCHITECTURE

Morning

Take U3, or hopper buses 2A or 3A, to Herrengasse/Michaelerplatz. After coffee at Demel (➤ 59, 67), turn right into Graben to St. Peter's Church (➤ 40), then head on to St. Stephen's Cathedral (➤ 43).
South of the cathedral, at Singerstrasse 7, is the Church and Treasury of the Teutonic Knights (Deutschordenshaus und-kirche).

Lunch

Zum Weissen Rauchfangkehrer
✉ Weihburggasse offers local specialties; for a fish lunch, go to Nordsee (➤ 65).

Afternoon

Visit the Capuchin Church and Crypt (➤ 42), then go to the Lobkowitz Palais and visit the Theater Museum (➤ 52, panel).
From the Augustinian Church (➤ 37), head east along Philharmonikerstrasse for coffee at the Hotel Sacher (➤ 84).

ITINERARY FOUR	THE OLD TOWN

Morning

Take U1 or U4 to Schwedenplatz. West, toward Morzinplatz, are the steps to St. Rupert's Church (➤ 51) and the Synagogue at Seitenstettengasse 4. Detour up Judengasse to the Hoher Markt and the Anchor Clock (main display at noon, ➤ 58).

Lunch

The Griechenbeisl ✉ Fleischmarkt 11 offers expensive but genuine Viennese fare.

Afternoon

Visit the Greek Orthodox Chapel ✉ Griechengasse 5 and Church of the Holy Trinity (Griechisch-orthodoxe Kirche H) ✉ Fleischmarkt 15. Down Fleischmarkt, turn right along Postgasse, past the Ukrainian Uniate Church of St. Barbara and the Dominican Church, then left into Bäckerstrasse and Dr-Ignaz-Seipel-Platz for the Academy of Sciences.
The Jesuitengasse beside Jesuitenkirche (➤ 50) brings you via Schönlaterngasse (left) to Heiligenkreuzerhof.

15

WALKS

Café on the Graben

THROUGH THE INNER CITY

Start at the Burgtor on the Ringstrasse. Walk through the Arch (Burgtor), which commemorates Napoleon's defeat, into the Heldenplatz. On your right stands the Neue Hofburg, containing museums and the National Library. Continue on through the Hofburg arches (► 35) into the main courtyard (In der Burg), where you'll find the entrance to the Imperial Apartments and, via the Swiss Gate (Sweizertor) on the south side, access to the Burgkapelle and the treasuries (Weltliche und Geistliche Schatzkammer). Continue through the Michaelertor onto Michaelerplatz, and turn right for Josefsplatz.

Head along Augustinerstrasse, past the Augustinian Church (► 37) and the Albertina (► 54) on the right. Turn left after Hotel Sacher into Kärntner Strasse, Vienna's premier shopping street. Turn right down Annagasse, past the baroque Annakirche (► 50), then left into Seilerstätte and left again into Himmelpfortgasse, passing the Winter Palace of Prince Eugene of Savoy (► 53).

At Kärntner Strasse again turn right and continue to Stephansplatz and St. Stephen's Cathedral (► 43). Opposite is the Haas-Haus (1990), by Hans Hollein. Its upper-floor café affords a fine view of the cathedral, which is ironic given that the building itself is controversial for having blocked that same view from the Graben. Walk west along the Graben past the Plague Column and St. Peter's Church (► 40). Continue west along picturesque Naglergasse to the southwestern edge of Am Hof.

Proceed along the Heidenschuss through the Freyung (► 38), and turn left through the Ferstel Arcade. Emerging on Herrengasse, walk back to the Hofburg's Michaelertor, or take U3 to Herrengasse.

THE SIGHTS

In the Hofburg (► 35)
- Imperial Apartments
- Secular and sacred treasuries
- Burgkapelle
- Spanish Riding School
- National Library

INFORMATION

Distance 2 miles
Time 2 hours without museums. Allow an extra 2½ hours for all
Start point Burgtor
- ⊞ G6
- 🚇 U1, U2, U4 Karlsplatz/Oper; tram stop: 1, 2 to Burgring
End point Michaelertor of the Hofburg
- ⊞ G6
- 🚇 U3
- 🍴 Self-service restaurant, Markt-Restaurant Rosenberger (✉ Maysedergasse 2, behind Sacher). Good cafés on Graben. Cafés in Haas-Haus and Naglergasse

THE RINGSTRASSE

Walk west from Schwedenplatz, then follow the Ring southward. On your right, in Schlickplatz, is the newly restored Rossauer Kaserne, originally a barracks built in "Windsor Castle style." Almost immediately on your left is Theophil Hansen's graceful Börse (Stock Exchange), a symphony of mellow red brickwork and silver-gray stone. Walk on through Schottentor: on your right are the Votivkirche (➤ 51) and the neo-Renaissance university, both by Heinrich Ferstel. On your left you pass the monument to Andreas von Liebenberg (who was mayor during the 1683 Turkish siege), before reaching the Burgtheater (➤ 31) and the new City Hall (➤ 30). Walk on past the Parliament (by Theophil Hansen) on your right; to the left is a park, the Volksgarten (➤ 56), in which are monuments to the Empress Elisabeth and Franz Grillparzer (Austria's greatest dramatic poet), and the mock-antique Theseum.

Continuing east on the Ring you pass the Natural History Museum (Naturhistorischer Museum), the Museum of Art History (➤ 32) and the monument to Maria Theresa (➤ 57). Pass Schillerplatz, with its statue of the poet and beyond that the Academy of Fine Arts (➤ 33), and continue until you reach the junction at Oper with the Opera House on your left.

Proceed along the right-hand side (southeast) of the Ring past the Hotel Imperial (➤ 84), where Hitler stayed, then past Schwarzen-bergplatz and into the Stadtpark (➤ 56). Leave the Stadtpark near the Museum of Applied Art (➤ 47). Cross the Ring to Georg-Coch-Platz and walk past Otto Wagner's Austrian Post Office Savings Bank (➤ 58), then follow the Ring round to the left and back to Schwedenplatz.

Statue of Pallas Athene in front of the Parliament

THE SIGHTS

- Börse
- Votivkirche (➤ 51)
- Vienna University
- Burgtheater (➤ 31)
- New City Hall (➤ 30)
- Parliament
- Volksgarten (➤ 56)

INFORMATION

Distance 2 miles
Time 2½ hours
Start and end point
    Schwedenplatz
🚇 H6
🚊 U1, U4
🚋 Tram 1, 2
🍴 Café Landtmann next to Burgtheater, favorite haunt of Sigmund Freud

EVENING STROLLS

INFORMATION

Geymüller-Schlössel

✉ Khevenhüllerstrasse 2,
Währing

☎ 479 3139

🕐 Mar–Oct: Mon–Wed
10:30–5; Thu–Sun by
appointment

🚃 Tram 41 to last stop

💶 Moderate

Safe city

Vienna remains one of the
world's safest cities. Whether you
are strolling through the suburbs
or walking in the old town during
the evening, you are unlikely to
be at risk. That said, lone
travelers should take sensible
precautions. The red-light district
has been restricted to the Gürtel
(Outer Ring Road) and is strictly
regulated.

In the Bermuda Triangle

FROM PÖTZLEINSDORF TO THE WINE VILLAGES

If you start mid- to late afternoon, there will be time for the delightful Pötzleinsdorfer Park (tram 41 from Schottentor to last stop). Nearby is the Empire-style Geymüller-Schlössel, with a collection of Biedermeier (1814–1848) furniture and Viennese clocks.

From the Schlössel, walk up Khevenhüllerstrasse over the hill, where Währing merges with the village of Neustift am Walde; here, and in the next village above (Salmannsdorf—walk up Keylwerthgasse), are Vienna's most attractive wine taverns. Atmospheric places with good wines are Fuhrgassl-Huber (➤ 64) and Zeiler.

Return on bus 35A from Neustift. Change at the Krottenbach/Silbergasse junction and take tram 38 to Schottentor.

THE BERMUDA TRIANGLE

The so-called Bermuda Triangle, reached by U1 or U4 to Schwedenplatz, roughly covers the area of an old Jewish quarter. During the evening the scene around the Seitenstettengasse, Ruprechtsplatz, and Judengasse is extremely lively: there are live-music bars—the Roter Engel (➤ 82) is the most famous—and other watering-holes and eateries such as Rasputin ✉ Seitenstettengasse 3, Relax ✉ Seitenstettengasse 5, and Krah Krah (➤ 83). The latter offers a vast choice of beers. There are also nightclubs aplenty in the area.

ORGANIZED SIGHTSEEING

Rambling in the Wienerwald (Vienna Woods) is a favorite Viennese pastime. The Information Bureau in the City Hall (Rathaus) dispenses maps with *Wanderwege* (routes for walkers). A good way to see Vienna between May and September is with a bike tour organized by Pedal Power ☎ 729 7234. The three-hour tour covers the main sights of the inner city (or the Danube Island and wine taverns). Bikes are provided. The meeting point is the Ferris wheel in the Prater (► 56).

Wienerwald

GUIDED WALKS
The Vienna Tourist Information Bureau ✉ Albertinaplatz 1 ☎ 513 8892 🕔 Daily 9–7 publishes a detailed pamphlet, updated every month. The choice of walks is constantly changing and may cover anything from "Vienna Underground" to Hundertwasser sights. For information in English ☎ 876 7111 or 774 8901; fax 774 8933

WORTHWHILE GUIDED TOURS
Vienna International Centre (UN organizations) ☎ 26060-3328 🕔 Mon–Fri 11AM, 2PM; Otto Wagner's Steinhof Church (► 24); the Augarten Porcelain Manufactory (► 72) ☎ 211 24-11

EXCURSIONS OUTSIDE VIENNA
Highly recommended are the River Danube trips organized by the DDSG-Blue Danube Schiffstundfahrten ✉ Schiffstation Reichsbrücke ☎ 588 80-0; fax 588 80-440. From April to October there are cruises through the Wachau wine region up to the monastery at Melk and events such as Halloween evening cruises at other times.

TOURS OF THE CITY
Two main operators are Vienna Sightseeing Tours ✉ Stelzhamergasse 4 ☎ 712 4683 and Cityrama Sightseeing ✉ Börsegasse 1 ☎ 534 13-0; mobile 0663 82 96 92. A city tour aboard an old-time tram starts from Otto Wagner Pavilion on Karlsplatz. Pre-booking required ☎ 7909 44026 🕔 May–Oct: Sat 11:30, 1:30; Sun and hols 9:30, 11:30, 1:30

Vienna on foot
Vienna's most intriguing sights are best visited on foot. Try a guided tour around the city or a ramble in the Wienerwald. Alternatively, public transportation is reliable. The modern subway has elevators at main stations only. There are good bus tours that take you to main attractions. The Vienna Card giving discounts at sights and on transportation can be obtained from the Vienna Tourist Bureau.

EXCURSIONS

INFORMATION

Heiligenkreuz
☎ 02258 8703-0
🚌 Bus 365 from
   Südtirolerplatz
🕐 Daily 10–5; tours 10AM,
   11AM

Mayerling
🚌 Bus 365 from
   Südtirolerplatz
🕐 The chapel: daily 10–12:30,
   1:30–4:45

Laxenburg
🚌 Bus 267 from
   Südtirolerplatz-Laxenburg
🚆 From Südbahnhof
🕐 Museum: Sun 10–noon
   (longer hours for
   exhibitions). Franzensburg:
   daily 10–noon, 2–5

Dürnstein
🚆 From Franz-Josefs-Bahnhof
🚢 Contact the DDSG at
   Handelskai 265 (☎ 727
   10-0 or 727 50-0)

HEILIGENKREUZ

This abbey, whose name "Holy Cross" is derived from the fragment of the True Cross preserved in a tabernacle on the main altar, was founded in 1133 by the Cistercians. The church has a lovely Gothic nave, and later baroque features include a Trinity Column (a Central European monument depicting the Holy Trinity, often commemorating a plague) in the courtyard.

MAYERLING

Mayerling is famous for the suicide in 1889 of Crown Prince Rudolf, whose liberal views deeply antagonized his father, Emperor Franz Joseph. On January 28, Rudolf and his 17-year-old mistress, Baroness Marie Vetsera, retired secretly to this Wienerwald hunting lodge; following a farewell dinner, Rudolf shot Marie and then himself. After the tragedy, Emperor Joseph ordered the lodge to be demolished and a neo-Gothic memorial chapel to be erected on the site.

LAXENBURG

About 9 miles south of Vienna is the moated 18th-century castle of Laxenburg. Highlights of this romantic folly are the Habsburg Hall of Fame and the re-creation of a medieval dungeon, complete with the model of a knight in chains.

DÜRNSTEIN

This attractive town is set on the edge of the wine-growing region of Wachau. Richard I (the Lion-heart) was imprisoned here in 1192. According to legend, his minstrel, Blondel, roamed Europe in search of him, playing outside castle windows until one day the king responded. The enormous ransom raised for the king's release was used to build up Vienna. The main feature of Dürnstein is the 18th-century monastery and church built by Matthias Steinl.

BADEN

A geological fault where the eastern edge of the Alps meets the Vienna Basin is responsible for the mineral springs at Baden, first exploited by the Romans. The now-sleepy town became a fashionable spa during the Beidermeier period (1815–1848). Mozart wrote his sublime *Ave Verum* chorus for the choir of the parish church here. The town is full of Joseph Kornhäusel's neo-Classical architecture (such as the Sauerhof and the Town Hall). A tram (Lokalbahn) runs from Oper all the way (15 miles) to Baden. There are operetta performances from July to mid-September and (also in September) a Beethoven festival.

GUMPOLDSKIRCHEN

Close to Baden (Road 12 southwest of Vienna) is the wine village of Gumpoldskirchen, whose main street is full of *Heurigen* (▶ 64). The region produces some good white wines (Zierfandler, Rotgipfler, and Neuburger).

Dürnstein Church and ruined castle

INFORMATION

Baden
- Lokalbahn (tram) from Oper
- Operetta performances
  Jul–mid-Sep

Gumpoldskirchen
- Road 12 from Vienna via Mödling
- Bus from Baden

Marie Vetsera's grave

Thirteen Babenbergs (the pre-Habsburg dynasty) are buried at Heiligenkreuz. Crown Prince Rudolf von Habsburg's lover, Baroness Marie Vetsera, lies in the abbey cemetery. After the tragic events at Mayerling (see main text), her dressed corpse was brought here at night, propped up in a carriage to avoid arousing suspicion.

WHAT'S ON

Performances, exhibitions, events, and lectures are listed in the monthly *Programm* from the Tourist Information Bureau. For movies, see the daily papers. German-speakers can also check the weekly *Falter*.

February	*Opernball* (last Thu of month): The Opera Ball is the highlight of the social calendar.
March	*Osterklang Wien*: New festival (founded 1997) celebrating the Wiener Philharmoniker and featuring world-famous soloists.
March–June & September–December	Equestrian ballet, performed by the Lipizzaners of the Spanish Riding School; performance times and tickets (▶ 36).
April	*Frühlingsfestival* (second week in Apr–mid-May): A series of concerts in the Musikverein and Konzerthaus.
May	*Maifest* (May 1): Celebrations mostly in the Prater. The traditional Socialist march through the town looks increasingly self-conscious.
	Spring Marathon (mid-May): From Schönbrunn to the Rathaus.
	Wiener Festwochen (early May to mid-Jun): This arts festival includes opera, plays, dances, exhibitions, and orchestras.
June	*Klangbogen Wien* (Jun–Sep): Chamber music and some jazz in attractive smaller venues such as the ballrooms of baroque palaces.
	Open-air festival (end Jun): Music, cabaret, and theater on the Danube Island (Donauinsel).
July	*Jazz Festival*: Jazz ensembles at the Opera House and the Volkstheater.
	Opera on Film (Jul–Aug): Opera movies on a giant screen in front of the Rathaus. Free open-air seating.
	Mozart at Schönbrunn (Jul–Aug): Mozart opera performed against a backdrop of the fake Roman ruins in the park at Schönbrunn.
October	*Vienna Film Festival Wien Modern* (Oct–Nov): One of the world's best festivals of contemporary music.
November–December	*Christkindlmarkt* (mid-Nov to Dec 24): A Christmas fair with dozens of stalls selling knickknacks and fun food of various kinds.
	"Mozart and Friends": Concert house series devoted to the works of Mozart and his contemporaries.
New Year	*Die Fledermaus*: Performances of Johann Strauss's operetta at the State Opera.

VIENNA's
top 25 sights

The sights are shown on the maps on the inside front cover and inside back cover, numbered **1–25** *from west to east across the city*

KIRCHE AM STEINHOF

INFORMATION

- ➕ A6
- ✉ Baumgartner Höhe 1, Penzing
- ☎ 91 060-11201
- 🕐 Organized tours (in German) Sat 3–4:30 or telephone for an appointment to visit
- 🚌 Buses 47A, 48A
- ♿ None
- 💰 Moderate (tours in German); expensive (tours in English)
- ❓ Telephone for times of tours in English

The weird and wonderful Steinhof Church was built by Otto Wagner for mental patients in 1907. The interior is clinically white with special fittings, full of wonders from Secession artists—most notably Kolo Moser's fabulous glass-mosaic windows.

Functionalism Great churches tend to be long on awe-inspiring atmosphere, and Wagner's church, appropriately, evokes sentiment. At the same time, it is functional, and provides aesthetic and religious equipment and tools necessary for dealing with people who are mentally ill.

Exterior features The facade is striking: the copper cupola, with its lovely patina, rises behind the two squared columns on which sit St. Leopold and St. Severin, patron saints of Lower Austria. The portico has four columns topped by massive copper angels by Othmar Schimkovitz in front of an impressive arched, stained-glass window.

The interior A number of features enhance the brightness of the light-flooded interior. A false ceiling in the cupola imitates a star-studded sky, and a vast, colorful glass mosaic covers the wall behind the altar, while Kolo Moser's windows in the crossing of the vault and above the side altars are also glass mosaic. The overall effect is luxurious, and yet Wagner's design is also highly functional. The short oak benches were positioned in a spacious semicircle to facilitate the removal of ill patients, and running water was used in the stoop to minimize the risk of infection. Attention was also paid to heating, ventilation, and acoustics.

SCHLOSS SCHÖNBRUNN

Schönbrunn is a cold if imposing palace, designed to show how many rooms a great monarch could afford. Yet Maria Theresa (1740–1780) made it a cheerful home for her 12 surviving children.

Pacassi's palace The original designs for an imperial residence in the hunting park with the beautiful spring (Schönbrunn) were made by Johann Bernhard Fischer von Erlach in 1695, and were intended to rival Versailles. Only part of it was built when, between 1744 and 1749, Maria Theresa's court architect, Nikolaus Pacassi, revamped the design. His symmetrical, immensely long palace is a vast corridor of gilded and crimson displays—Japanese, Italian, Persian, and Indian works of art, ceiling frescoes celebrating the Habsburgs, and 18th-century furniture and porcelain. The palace looks out on a park with immaculate parterres and hedges and a vista of ornamental pools and fountains.

The park The 18th-century gardens were later partially restyled by Adrian van Steckhoven in the romantic manner. The modern park now also contains a spectacular glass and iron palm house and a zoo.

HIGHLIGHTS

- Coach museum (right of main entrance)
- Chapel with fresco by Daniel Gran
- Oriental panels, Vieux-Lacque Room
- Mirrors and frescoed ceiling in Great Gallery
- Indian and Persian miniatures
- Imperial embroidery
- Chinoiserie
- Trompe-l'œil landscapes
- Stucco by Fischer von Erlach

INFORMATION

- ✠ C/D9/10
- ✉ Schönbrunner Schlosstrasse 47
- ☎ 81 113-239
- 🕐 Palace Apr 1–Oct 30: daily 8:30–5. Oct 31–Mar 31: 8:30–4:30. Coach museum 9–6:30. Zoo summer: 9–6:30; winter 9–sunset. Park 6–sunset
- 🍴 Café and Tyrolean Restaurant
- 🚇 Schönbrunn
- 🚌 Bus 10A; trams 10, 58
- ♿ Good
- 💵 Tour: expensive
- ❓ Palace can be visited only on hourly tours. Grand Tour (40 rooms); Imperial Tour (22 rooms). Occasional concerts; performances in Shlosstheater

Schlosstheater, Schönbrunn

25

3

THE NARRENTURM

You may find it bizarre or gruesome but you won't forget a visit to this 18th-century, circular Fool's Tower, now home to a museum. Be prepared for its medical chamber of horrors.

HIGHLIGHTS

- 1820s apothecary's shop
- Specimens in formaldehyde
- Abnormal skeletons
- Diseased lungs
- The world's best kidney and gallstone collection

INFORMATION

- ✚ G5
- ✉ Spitalgasse 2, then follow signs to Courtyard 13
- ☎ 406 8672
- 🕔 Sep–Jul: Wed 3–6; Thu 8–11; first Sat of month 10–1. Closed Aug
- Ⓢ Schottentor
- 🚋 Trams 5, 43, 44
- ♿ None
- 💰 Moderate
- ❓ Tours by arrangement

Utopian design The Narrenturm is a strange cylindrical building with a circular inner court-yard divided in half by an extra wing. It was built by Isidore Canevale in 1784 on the orders of Emperor Joseph II, who had also founded the Vienna General Hospital in the same grounds. Each of its five floors had 28 centrally heated cells for mental patients, called fools in the parlance of the day; however, not everyone here was actually mad. The emperor reprimanded one aristocrat, Count Seilern, for shutting his son in here because the young man refused to wed the bride selected for him.

Piece of cake The Viennese have always had an irreverent attitude to the Fool's Tower, calling it the Emperor Joseph's *Gugelhupf* because it is supposed to resemble the locally prized pound cake. Unpopular politicians with ill-thought-out policies are often said to "belong in the *Gugelhupf*."

Museum The Narrenturm was used as an asylum until 1866; subsequently it housed a store and provided living quarters for medical staff. It is now the Museum for Pathological Anatomy, and contains a large collection of medical curiosities, many of them somewhat gruesome.

Aesculapian snake on museum door

JOSEPHINUM

In these rooms aspiring military surgeons pored over life-like anatomical wax models, preparing for a career on the battlefields of the Empire. Their intention was humanitarian—Joseph II had seen first hand the terrible suffering caused by medical ineptitude.

Wax models The museum for the history of medicine, commonly called the Josephinum after its founder Emporer Joseph II, was a pioneering institution in Austria. No expense was spared in providing teaching materials. The most impressive of these are the 1,200 wax models used for teaching anatomy. They were made between 1775 and 1785 in Florence under the direction of Felice Fontana and Paolo Mascagni, and are considered the finest examples of this obscure form of educational art outside Florence itself.

Other collections Teaching ceased in the 19th century. In 1920 Max Neuburger's medical collection was added to the wax models. The present collection includes memorabilia of Semmelweis, Billroth, and other famous surgeons, as well as mememtoes of Sigmund Freud. Since 1996 the world's largest museum of endoscopy has been here also.

Gates Leaving the neoclassical building by its splendid wrought-iron gate you shortly reach Strudlhofgasse, which leads to the double-flighted Strudlhofstiege (Strudlhof Steps). This graceful art-nouveau stairway with lanterns and wells was designed in 1910 by Theodor Jäger. The steps are especially attractive at night, when the stairway lanterns throw a soft light on the silvery stone.

HIGHLIGHTS

- Fine wrought-iron gates
- Library with coffered ceiling and Corinthian columns
- Anatomical wax figures by Felice Fontana
- Memorabilia of great surgeons
- Collection of medical instruments
- Endoscopy museum

INFORMATION

- ✚ G5
- ✉ Währinger Strasse 25
- ☎ 4277-63401
- 🕐 Mon–Fri 9–3
- 🚊 Trams 37, 38, 40, 41, 42 from Schottentor
- 🚶 Moderate
- ↔ The Narrenturm (➤ 26)
- ❓ Tours on request in advance

5

SERVITENKIRCHE

The Servite Church is closely associated with the Servite St. Peregrine. Peregrine bread rolls are sold all over Vienna from April 6 to May 6, ever since a local baker honored this saint (who gave bread to the poor) by contributing some of his wares to the same cause.

HIGHLIGHTS

- Wrought-iron screen (1675)
- Death of St. Juliana Falconieri sculpture
- Martyrdom of St. John Nepomuk sculpture
- Lourdes grotto
- Cupola with frescoes of Assumption/Crowning of Mary
- B. Moll's carved pulpit
- 15th-century crucifix
- Rococo ironwork

Cupola frescoes

INFORMATION

- ✚ G5
- ✉ Servitengasse 9
- ☎ 317 6195-0
- 🕐 Daily 8AM–10PM
- Ⓜ U4 Rossauer Lände
- 🚋 Tram D
- ♿ Access easy
- 🎟 Free

Origins of the church Emperor Ferdinand II allowed the Servite nuns to settle in Vienna in the 17th century. Their church was begun in 1656, outside the city walls, to a design by Carlo Canevale; but the money ran out on the death of the order's patron, the imperial general Ottavio Piccolomini. The rich and exciting interior decoration was completed in 1677. The church is an impressive example of a baroque design that predates the second Turkish siege of 1683. It was also the city's first church to contain an oval nave.

Church interior Most of the superb stucco work is by Giovanni Bussi and Giovanni Barbarino. Upon entering the church you will see fabulous stuccolustro chapels to the right and left under the towers; the sculptures show respectively the death of St. Juliana Falconieri, who founded the Servite order, and the martyrdom of St. John Nepomuk, a vicar-general of Prague who was drowned in the Vltava river by order of King Wenceslas IV.

St. Peregrine Off the main church to the right is the chapel of St. Peregrine. He suffered from foot ailments, and his shrine has traditionally attracted the similarly afflicted—among them the composer Joseph Haydn.

SIGMUND FREUD MUSEUM

Some of this century's most influential ideas came from the tenant of apartment No. 5, Berggasse 19. Whether you think of Freud as a cantankerous authoritarian or as a genius, it is interesting to see the place where his work began.

Sigmund Freud 1856–1939 Internationally famous and recognized as the founder of modern psychoanalysis, Freud was none the less typically Viennese, playing tarock (a card game still popular with the older generation), visiting Café Landtmann (► 59), and taking a daily constitutional along the entire length of the Ringstrasse. Like many other gifted Jewish Viennese, Freud opted for medicine, partly because it was a profession in which discrimination was not the barrier that it could be in the army and bureaucracy. He pursued a career at the University of Vienna, where he became an Associate Professor in 1902.

Theories Freud's most controversial theory was that infantile sexual impulses were at the root of adult neuroses. Adler and Jung—the other famous early psychoanalysts, and contemporaries of Freud's—parted company with him over this. However, many now-mainstream concepts started with Freud—for example, division of the personality into id and ego, and the ideas of sublimation and the Oedipus complex. Although many academics still accept Freud's dogmas as axiomatic, his critics believe that he doctored his evidence. For them, doctrinaire psychoanalytic theory is the most stupendous intellectual confidence trick of the 20th century. The Viennese writer Karl Kraus, also a contemporary of Freud's, remarked: "Psychoanalysis is the disease of which it purports to be the cure."

HIGHLIGHTS

- Freud's hat and cane
- Antiquities collected by Freud on his travels
- Photographs of Freud and contemporaries
- Part of Freud's book collection
- Original writings
- Video room

Freudiana elsewhere

- Bust of Freud in Vienna University's courtyard
- Plaque at the picturesque spot where the role of dreams first occurred to Freud (✉ Bellevue Höhe, Himmelstrasse, 19th District 🚌 Buses 38A and 39A, both to last stop)

INFORMATION

- ➕ G5
- ✉ Berggasse 19
- ☎ 319 1596
- 🕐 Jul–Sep: daily 9–6. Oct–Jun: daily 9–4
- Ⓜ U2 Schottentor
- 🚊 Tram D
- ♿ Few
- 🎫 Moderate

NEUES RATHAUS

HIGHLIGHTS

Outside, in Rathauspark
- Statues of Babenberg rulers 976–1246
- Monument to Socialist Chancellor/President Karl Renner
- Opera movies in summer; Christmas Fair (Christkindl-markt) in winter

Inside
- The Arkadenhof (arcaded coutyard)
- *Festsaal*
- Roter Salon (mayor's reception room)
- Council chamber
- Senate chamber
- Heraldic rooms

INFORMATION

- G6
- Friedrich-Schmidt-Platz 1
- 52 550
- Tours: Mon–Fri 1PM; or phone to book
- Rathauskeller or Café Sluka
- U2 Rathaus
- Trams 1 and 2 on the Ringstrasse, D, J
- Few
- Tour: moderate
- Burgtheater (➤ 31)
- Visits by tour only (apply at Schmidthalle). The Rathaus is a starting point for other tours, a general information center, and a concert venue

Bust of President Karl Renner in Rathauspark

The "new" City Hall (Neues Rathaus), built between 1872 and 1883, is perhaps the finest neo-Gothic building in all Vienna. The debating chamber would not disgrace a small independent nation.

Inspiration for the Rathaus The great buildings along the Ringstrasse, built between the 1860s and 1880s, exemplify the values of Liberalism—industrial modernization, democracy, and capitalist enterprise. It is typically Viennese that this vision of the future was expressed in historic symbols. Architect Friedrich Schmidt chose, as his model for the Rathaus, the town halls typical of medieval Flanders.

The facade The massive facade, with its traceried arches over the arcades, looks onto the Ringstrasse; above the arches are graceful loggias and imposing balustrades adorned with statues. Rising from the center is the dramatic 325-foot tower topped by an 11-foot copper statue.

The interior The grand staircases, noble promenades, and richly decorated halls are a dizzying spectacle; most notable are the City Council Chamber and the Festsaal (Ceremonial Hall).

BURGTHEATER

The heavily subsidized Burgtheater is Austria's national theater in all but name. Productions of coruscating plays by Thomas Bernhard (d1989), ridiculing Austria's complacency and exposing its half-submerged Nazi past, provoked all the outrage the author anticipated.

Origins The name is taken from the court theater that stood on the edge of the Hofburg (on Michaelerplatz) from the time of Maria Theresa (1741) until 1888. Mozart's *Marriage of Figaro* was premièred there in 1786.

Architecture This neo-Renaissance building by Karl von Hasenauer and Gottfried Semper opened in 1888, but it was soon altered; so much attention in the design had been paid to architectural proportion and so little to function that some of the boxes faced away from the stage and the acoustics were appalling. An anecdote at the time claimed that "In the Parliament you can't hear anything, in the Rathaus you can't see anything and in the Burgtheater you can neither see nor hear anything."

Decorative plan Inside and out, the Burgtheater is a symbolic celebration of the history of drama from ancient times. On the central facade are monuments to the world's greatest playwrights. On the ceremonial stairways that rise through the two wings toward the auditorium are busts of the great Austrian and German dramatists whose works are performed here. Gustav Klimt, his brother Ernst, and Franz Matsch decorated the ceilings above the stairway with frescoes depicting the history of theater. Oil portraits of famous Viennese actors and actresses hang along the walls of the curving first-floor foyer.

HIGHLIGHTS

Exterior
- View from the Rathaus across Ringstrasse
- Busts of famous dramatists
- Frieze of Dionysius and Ariadne
- Apollo and the Muses of Comedy and Tragedy

Interior
- Ceremonial stairway, busts of dramatists
- *Thespiskarren*, Gustav Klimt
- *Globe Theatre, London*, Gustav Klimt
- *Theatre at Taormina*, Gustav Klimt
- *Medieval Mystery Theatre*, Ernst Klimt
- *Molière's Le Malade Imaginaire*, Ernst Klimt

INFORMATION

- ✠ G6
- ✉ Dr-Karl-Lueger-Ring
- ☎ 51444-4145
- 🕐 Guided tours daily (telephone for times). Closed Dec 24, Good Friday, and Jul and Aug except for tours
- Ⓤ U2 Schottentor
- 🚋 Trams 1 and 2 on the Ringstrasse
- ♿ Good
- 🎫 Moderate
- ↔ Neues Rathaus (➤ 30)
- ❓ Visits by tour only

KUNSTHISTORISCHES MUSEUM

HIGHLIGHTS

- *Theseus and Centaur,* Antonio Canova
- *The Apotheosis of the Renaissance,* Mihály Munkácsy
- Hans Makart's allegories of art above the stairwell

In the collections

- 2,000 BC blue faience hippopotamus, Egyptian Collection
- *Gemma Augustea,* Roman imperial cameo
- Cellini gold salt cellar
- *Madonna in the Meadow,* Raphael
- *Conversion of St. Paul,* Francesco Parmigianino
- *Infanta Margareta Teresa,* Velázquez
- *The Tower of Babel,* Brueghel

INFORMATION

- G6/7
- Maria-Theresien-Platz/Burgring 5
- 52 524-403/404
- Tue–Wed, Fri–Sun 10–6; Thu 10–9. Closed May 1, Nov 1
- Café upstairs
- U2 Babenberger Strasse, Volkstheater
- Trams 1 and 2 on the Ringstrasse D, J
- Good
- Moderate
- Frequent lectures and special exhibitions

Here in the Museum of Art History you'll find the Habsburgs' fabulous art collection, acquired over five centuries (especially by emperors Friedrich III and Rudolf II, and archdukes Leopold Wilhelm and Ferdinand II). However, it's virtually impossible to see all of it in a day.

Origins The German architect Gottfried von Semper planned to continue the sweep of the Neue Hofburg and build a parallel wing on the other side of the Heldenplatz; both wings were to extend across the Ringstrasse, creating a gigantic Imperial Forum of museums. The Museum of Art History and the Natural History Museum facing it are the partial realization of this attempt to bring together the widely dispersed Habsburg treasures. The Museum of Art History contains collections of paintings, Egyptian artifacts, sculpture, decorative art, coins, and medals.

Architectural decoration Both the Museum of Art History and the Natural History Museum opposite are principally the work of Gottfried von Semper; their interiors are by Karl Hasenauer. Between the museums lies a park that is dominated by a monument to Maria Theresa (1740–1780). Inside the Museum of Art History, marble and stucco are interspersed with murals; most notably the main staircase is decorated by Hans Makart with allegorical frescoes in praise of art. Note the dome, which has medallions of collector-emperors. Hasenauer planned showrooms appropriate to their contents; the Egyptian collection, for example, is ornamented with columns from Luxor, a present from the Khedive to the Emperor Franz Josef.

AKADEMIE DER BILDENDEN KÜNSTE

In 1907, Adolf Hitler was denied entry to the Academy of Fine Arts for his poor rendering of human heads. When he tried a second time, he was rejected by the academy's Professor of Architecture, Otto Wagner, because he lacked the requisite high-school qualifications. He later turned to politics.

The building The academy was completed in 1876 by one of the greatest architects of the Ringstrassen era, Theophil Hansen, whose other work includes the classical Parliament, the Stock Exchange, and numerous neo-Renaissance palaces. In the middle of the square in front is a statue of the poet Friedrich Schiller (1759–1805). Along the facade are figures from antiquity associated with the fine arts; on the back are allegorical frescoes by August Eisenmenger, the academy's Professor for Painting in the late 19th century. Founded in 1692 by the painter Peter von Strudel, the academy numbers among its alumni the painter Friedensreich Hundertwasser, whose spectacular multi-colored house at Löwengasse, 3rd District is a tourist attraction, and Fritz Wotruba, designer of an extraordinary modern church (▶ 51).

The interior Anselm Feuerbach's ceiling fresco, *Downfall of Titans*, dominates the Basilical Hall; the collection of Dutch Masters is renowned, and the graphic art collection is superb.

HIGHLIGHTS

- *Last Judgement*, Heironymus Bosch
- *Views of Venice*, Antonio Guardi
- *Self-Portrait*, Brent Fabritius
- *Family in a Courtyard*, Pieter de Hooch
- *Sketches for Banqueting House, Whitehall*, Rubens

INFORMATION

- ✚ G7
- ✉ Schillerplatz 3
- ☎ 5881 6225-230
- 🕐 Tue–Sun 10–4. Closed May 1, Corpus Christi and the following Fri, Nov 1–2
- Ⓜ U1, U2, U4 Karlsplatz/Oper
- 🚊 Trams 1 and 2 on the Ringstrasse
- ♿ Few
- 💰 Moderate

Statue at the Academy of Fine Arts

11

SECESSION BUILDING

HIGHLIGHTS

- Three gorgons over the doorway
- Inscription *Ver Sacrum* (Sacred Spring)
- Dome of gilded laurel leaves
- Picturesque sculpted owls
- Vast flower tubs on tortoise stands
- Statue: *Mark Antony in a Chariot Drawn by Lions* (1900), Arthur Strasser
- *Beethoven Frieze* (1902), Gustav Klimt

INFORMATION

- ✚ G7
- ✉ Friedrichstrasse 12
- ☎ 587 5307
- 🕐 Tue–Sun 10–6 (Thu until 8)
- 🍴 Summer café beside the building
- Ⓜ U1, U2, U4 Karlsplatz
- 🚌 Bus 59A
- ♿ Few
- 💷 Inexpensive
- ↔ Akademie der Bildenden Künste (➤ 33), Karlskirche (➤ 44)

In a pointed gesture of defiance towards the art establishment, this exhibition building of revolutionary design was built right under the windows of the Academy of Fine Arts. Their motto is inscribed over the main entrance: "To every age its art, to art its freedom."

Vienna Secession In 1897, frustrated with the increasing conservatism of academic painting in Vienna and its stranglehold over the art market, a group of young artists broke away to form the subsequently famous "Vienna Secession." The elected head of the Vienna Secession was the painter Gustav Klimt, whose *Beethoven Frieze*—an allegorical interpretation of the themes of the Ninth Symphony conceived as a homage to the composer—can be seen here.

Jugendstil Like other artists of the day, Klimt had begun his career working in the conventional genre of historical painting (exemplified by his work for the Burgtheater, ➤ 31). The Secession's style was associated with Jugendstil, the German version of art nouveau. It is sensuous and decorative, and achieves its best effects in architecture and stained glass (➤ 58).

The exhibition hall The breakaway artists needed a hall both to exhibit their own works and to show avant-garde art from abroad. In 1898, Joseph Maria Olbrich completed the cube-like, towered, and windowless Secession Building with a glass roof that supplied daylight. The Viennese dubbed it the "golden cabbage" because of its gilded dome of entwined laurel leaves. Inside, innovative, movable partitions make the display space more flexible.

HOFBURG

It is said that the Habsburgs never finished their great projects; the Hofburg (the former imperial residence), like St. Stephen's Cathedral (▶ 43) and the Habsburg Empire itself, is an example of their unfinished business.

Ages of the Hofburg The first fortress was built in 1275 on the site that later became the Schweizerhof. This building is named after the 18th-century Swiss Guards at the Burg and, with the Schweizertor (Swiss Gate), is the oldest surviving section of the Hofburg, built in the mid-16th century. The other Renaissance wings are the Amalienburg and, to the north, the beautiful Stallburg, where the famous dancing horses, the Lipizzaners, are stabled.

Baroque Much of the richest architecture is 17th- and 18th-century baroque. Italian architects built the wing named after Emperor Leopold I (Leopoldinischer Trakt) in 1681. Under Charles VI and Maria Theresa, Johann Bernhard Fischer von Erlach and his son, Josef Emanuel, worked on the sumptuous Hofbibliothek (the Court, now National Library; 1726) and the Reitschule (1735, ▶ 36). Their rival, Lukas von Hildebrandt, began the Reichskanzleitrakt, which housed the officials of the Holy Roman Empire. It was altered and completed by Fischer von Erlach in 1730.

19th and 20th centuries The area bordering Michaelerplatz, which includes the State Apartments, was built in the 19th century to an earlier design in baroque style. The huge Neue Hofburg was finished only in 1913, shortly before the demise of the dynasty itself. It was to have been part of the Imperial Forum devised by Gottfried von Semper (▶ 32).

HIGHLIGHTS

- Burgkapelle (chapel)
- Schatzkammer (Treasury)
- Leopoldinischer Trakt
- State Apartments
- Prunksaal in Hofbibliothek
- Habsburg statues in domed hall of Hofbibliothek

INFORMATION

- ➕ G6
- ✉ State Apartments: Innere Burghof, Kaisertor. Hofibibliothek, Burgkapelle: Josefsplatz 1
- ☎ 532 1680
- 🕐 State Apartments 9–5. Library May–Oct: Mon–Wed, Fri, Sat 10–4; Thu 10–7; Sun and hols 10–2. Nov–Apr: Mon–Sat 10–2. Treasury Mon, Wed–Sun 10–6. Closed May 1, Nov 1. Burgkapelle Tue–Thu 1:30–3:30; Fri 1–3; mass Sun and church hols 9:15AM (obtain tickets Fri before). Vienna Boys Choir Sep–Jun
- 🚇 U3 Herrengasse
- 🚌 Hopper 3A to Habsburgergasse
- ♿ Few
- 💰 Expensive (where charged)
- ↔ Spanische Reitschule (▶ 36), Augustinerkirche (▶ 37), Michaelerkirche (▶ 51)
- ❓ Tours of State Apartments daily on the hour 10–4

13

SPANISCHE REITSCHULE

- Ceiling, best seen from top balcony
- Emperor's box at north end
- *Portrait of Karl VI*, Johann Georg Hamilton
- Riders' uniforms in the Vorführungen
- Horses' gold-braided manes and tails

Movements in the *haute école*

- *Capriole*: a leap into the air in which the hind legs are extended at the height of the jump
- *Levade*: the horse rears up in a slow, controlled manner
- *Piaffe*: trotting on the spot, often between two pillars
- *Croupade*: a leap with the legs tucked under the body

INFORMATION

- G6
- Josefsplatz
- Performances Feb–Jun, Sep–Oct: Sun 10:45AM and some evenings. "Morning training" Mon–Fri 10–12. Closed public hols
- 533 9031
- U3 Herrengasse
- Hopper 3A to Habsburgergasse
- Few
- Expensive
- Hofburg (➤ 35), Michaelerkirche (➤ 51)
- Tickets for morning training: purchase on the day at Josefsplatz 2, Gate 2

The "airs above the ground," the ancient practice of cavalry skills in which the horses were trained to fight by leaping and kicking at their riders' commands, are still rehearsed here in the baroque Spanish Riding School.

The building The Reitschule was constructed in 1735 by Josef Emanuel Fischer von Erlach for the father of Maria Theresa, Karl VI. Inside, two viewing galleries supported on columns ring the all-white space where the all-white Lipizzaner horses perform. It is called the Spanish Riding School because the horses originally came from Spain; the stud, established in 1580 at Lipica in Slovenia, gave its name to the Lipizzaners.

The performance The horses dance the quadrille, the gavotte, and the latest addition to their repetoire, the Viennese waltz showing the *haute école*, the most refined dressage techiques, which are derived from the battle tactics of the Middle Ages. The *Capriole* is a leap into the air in which the hind legs are extended at the height of the jump. In the *Levade* the horse rears up in a slow, controlled manner. In the *Piaffe* the horse trots on the spot, and in the *Croupade* the horse leaps with its legs tucked up under its body.

Popular The performances (*Vorführungen*) are very popular and are often reserved long in advance. If you haven't made a reservation you may be able to watch the morning training session (*Morgenarbeit*) instead. Although there is no music, and the chandeliers used during performances remain unlit, the training session still shows the horses in action and the beauty of the Winter Riding School itself.

AUGUSTINERKIRCHE

The historic Church of St. Augustine, the "parish church" of the Habsburg court, can seem bleak and forbidding. In its Loreto Chapel are preserved the hearts of members of the imperial family. On Sundays Vienna's best-sung masses cheer things up.

Origins The Gothic church is said to have been founded by Friedrich "the Handsome" of Habsburg (1289–1330) in fulfillment of a vow he made when imprisoned by the Bavarian king. In the Counter-Reformation, the Augustinians of the adjacent monastery formed the *Totenbrüderschaft* (Brotherhood of the Dead), which visited prisoners and buried executed criminals. A famous Augustinian was the fiery preacher Abraham a Sancta Clara (1644–1709), who criticized the Viennese for their licentiousness in sermons that were liberally sprinkled with violent images and anti-Semitism. The pulpit stands on the spot from which he preached.

Architectural features The original clock in the tower was a gift from the Hungarian Count Nadasdy, who lived in the house opposite and thought it would be convenient to check the time from his window.

Interior The interior was "re-gothicised" by Ferdinand von Hohenberg in the late 18th century. Notable features are the marble cenotaph (1805) by Antonio Canova for Marie Christine, the favorite daughter of Maria Theresa (1740–1780), and the rococo organ on which Brückner composed his Mass no.3. The St. George Chapel is dedicated to a Habsburg order similar to the Teutonic Knights and is the burial place of distinguished servants of the dynasty.

HIGHLIGHTS

- Clock tower
- Canova's tomb for Marie Christine
- Baroque pews
- Pulpit marking where Abraham a Sancta Clara preached
- Silver urns with Habsburg hearts, in Loreto Chapel
- "Supererogation Statue" for dedicating relics
- Graves of Habsburg dignitaries

Art from dissolved churches
- *Vision of Mary Magdalene*, J.M. Rottmayr
- Stucco figures of Sts. Augustine and Ambrose
- *Deposition from the Cross*, Johann Auerbach

INFORMATION

- ✚ G/H6
- ✉ Augustinerstrasse 3
- ☎ 533 7099
- 🕐 Mon–Sat 10–6; Sun 1–6 (and for morning sung mass)
- 🍴 Ancient Augustinerkeller, adjacent
- Ⓜ U1, U2, U4 Oper/Karlsplatz
- 🚌 Hopper 3A to Albertinaplatz
- ♿ None
- 💲 Free
- ↔ Hofburg (► 35)

FREYUNG

Freyung
- Section of medieval cobbles in the northeast corner
- Hildebrandt's Palais Kinsky, Freyung 4
- Austria Fountain, symbolizing major rivers of Habsburg lands

Schottenkirche and Prelacy Museum
- Gothic wing altar, Master of the Scots 1469–1480
- *Assumption*, Tobias Pock, and *St. Sebastian*, Joachim von Sandart
- High altar (Ferstel) with glass mosaic
- Tomb of Count Starhemberg

Palais Ferstel
- Danube Fountain

INFORMATION

- ✚ G6
- ✉ Schottenkirche and Prelacy Museum: Freyung 6. Palais Ferstel: Freyung 2
- ☎ Schottenkirche: 534 9820. Museum: 534 98600
- ◷ Schottenkirche usually 7AM–9PM. Museum Thu–Sat 10–5; Sun noon–5
- 🍴 Café Central in Palais Ferstel
- Ⓤ U2 Schottentor
- 🚍 Hopper 1A
- ♿ Few
- 🎟 Inexpensive

This irregularly shaped square acquired its name (meaning "asylum") as a result of its association with the adjacent Benedictine monastery, which until 1848 had the right to give asylum to fugitives from justice.

Freyung Eighteenth-century paintings show a lively scene, with stallholders, jugglers, and clowns. Baroque palaces still rim the square.

Schottenkirche The Abbey Church of the "Schotten" Benedictines, dominating the east side of the square, was called Scottish because the Latin name for Ireland was *Scotia maior*. The 15th-century Gothic altarpiece, now in the Prelacy Museum in the Schottenstift, shows the earliest extant view of Vienna.

Palais Ferstel This structure, on the south side of the square, is not actually a palace but a complex named after its architect. Inside, a glass-roofed arcade with gift shops leads from the Freyung to Herrengasse ("Street of the Lords"). Formerly the seat of The Vienna Stock Exchange.

OBIZZI PALACE

This picturesque little palace, on a side-street behind Am Hof, once belonged to Count Ernst Rüdiger von Starhemberg, who defended the city during the Turkish siege of 1683. As battles raged outside, lead cannonballs were cast in its fireplace.

History of the palace There was a dwelling here in the 11th century, possibly the successor to a Roman building. The irregular shape of the palace earned it the nickname "Harp House." The Starhembergs owned it for over a century from 1580 and added a story. The baroque facade and another floor were added by Ferdinand Obizzi, who commanded the city militia in 1690. Narrowly escaping demolition in 1901, it was repurposed as home of a clock museum on an order from the city council in 1917.

The Clock Museum (Uhrenmuseum) The first of its kind in the world, this museum covers three floors and houses more than 3,000 exhibits from the 15th to the 20th centuries. Many are unique, including an amazingly complicated astronomical clock—one of its hands requires 20,904 years to make one complete revolution.

HIGHLIGHTS

- Courtyard fountain with Roman trough
- Mechanism of the clock from the Old Town Hall
- Augsburg standing clock
- Nürnberg sand clock
- Onion clock by Isaac Roberts
- Astronomical clock
- Hussar-figure clock
- Rowboat clock
- Clock set in a picture of a landscape with waterfall
- Clock in the form of a bicycle

INFORMATION

- 🞧 H6
- ✉ Schulhof 2 (alley flanking Am Hof church)
- ☎ 533 2265
- 🕐 Tue–Sun 9–4:30
- Ⓜ U1, U3 Stephansplatz
- 🚌 Hopper 2A
- ♿ None
- 💶 Moderate
- ❓ Tours (minimum 8 persons)

PETERSKIRCHE

HIGHLIGHTS

- Relief of Charlemagne refounding St. Peter's
- Statues of the four apostles
- Sculptures of Faith, Hope, and Charity
- *Assumption of the Virgin*, J.M. Rottmayr
- Illusionist architecture by Galli-Bibiena
- Matthias Steinl's pulpit
- *Martyrdom of St. John Nepomuk*, Lorenzo Mattielli
- *Healing of the Lame Man*, Martino Altomonte
- Statues of Constantine and Charlemagne

INFORMATION

- H6
- Petersplatz 6
- 636 433
- Mon–Fri 6AM–6:30PM; Sat–Sun 7:30AM–6:30PM
- U1, U3 Stephansplatz
- Hopper 2A
- None
- Free
- The Stephansdom (▶ 43)

The most striking aspect of the lovely baroque St. Peter's Church is the way the two architects, Gabriele Montani and Lukas von Hildebrandt, fitted it into a space so narrow that it looks almost as if it had been poured into a mold.

Origins of the church It is thought that the first Christian sanctuary of Vienna (then Vindobona) was built on this site in late Roman times. A 1906 marble plaque on the east wall outside attributes the refounding of the church to Charlemagne, but this is not true. Because of St. Peter's historical significance, the Emperor Leopold I took a personal interest in the building of a new church on this site; he was present at the laying of the foundation stone in 1702, when a trench collapsed injuring members of the imperial retinue. Hildebrandt took over Montani's work shortly afterward, and Franz Jänggl extended the choir and completed the towers between 1730 and 1733.

The interior The external effect of compression and harmonious unity is continued in the interior, which is subordinated to the 123-foot diameter dome. There is striking ornamentation; note the trompe-l'œil effects in the choir by Antonio Galli-Bibiena, who was famous for his illusionist stage settings. Gilded stucco to the right as you face the altar depicts the martyrdom of St. John Nepomuk, a saint venerated in Central Europe. No less dazzling is the pulpit by Matthias Steinl. All the theatricality of high baroque art is exuberantly manifested here.

The exterior Niches on the facade show statues of the apostles, and the inscription above the middle door reads: "What I vow to the Lord for my salvation that will I fulfil."

ALTES RATHAUS

Once a private house, the Old City Hall was confiscated after an unsuccessful anti-Habsburg uprising and donated to the city council in 1316. The Habsburg dynasty continually suppressed the civic rights of the Viennese up to the 19th century.

The price of dissent Until 1309 the building was owned by Otto Haymo. After he led an unsuccessful anti-Habsburg uprising, Duke Friedrich "the Handsome" confiscated the house and seven years later it was given to the city.

History Several extensions of the hall were added during the 14th and 15th centuries. Its Gothic core dates from 1457. At the end of the 17th century it acquired baroque elements, most notably the facade, which shows the influence of Johann Bernhard Fischer von Erlach. The Vienna Council last sat in this building in 1885. It is now mostly municipal offices and the Bezirksmuseum (District Museum) for the 1st District, the old town (Innenstadt).

Sights in and around The baroque facade of the former Bohemian Court Chancellery across the street at Wipplingerstrasse 7 was mainly the work of Johann Bernhard Fischer von Erlach in 1714. Upstairs in the City Hall (Stiege 3) is the Museum of Austrian Resistance (during World War II), with its archive. In a courtyard is Georg Raphael Donner's *Andromeda Fountain*. At the rear, in Salvatorgasse, is a fine Renaissance portal to the Salvatorkapelle (the Chapel of the Savior); originally the City Hall chapel, it now belongs to the Old Catholic Community—those who rejected the 1870 doctrine of papal infallibility.

HIGHLIGHTS

Old City Hall
- Portals with J.M. Fischer's 1781 allegories
- Relief with city coat of arms, corner Stoss in Himmel
- Alberto Camesina's baroque stucco, 1713
- Museum of Austrian Resistance
- Old Town District Museum
- *Andromeda Fountain*, Georg Raphael Donner, in courtyard
- Renaissance doorway to Salvatorkapelle

Bohemian Chancellery
- Baroque portals with Atlas figures
- Coats of arms of Bohemia, Moravia, and Silesia on wall
- Lorenzo Mattielli's allegorical figures

INFORMATION

- ✚ H6
- ✉ Wipplingerstrasse 6–8
- ☎ 53436-01779
- 🕐 City Hall Mon, Wed, Sat 9AM–11AM; Sun 10–noon. Museum of Austrian Resistance Mon, Wed–Thu 9–5. District museum Wed, Fri 3–5
- 🚇 U1, U4 Schwedenplatz
- 🚌 Hopper 3A
- ♿ None
- 🍴 Moderate

41

KAPUZINERGRUFT

INFORMATION

- ✚ H6
- ✉ Tegetthoffstrasse 2
- ☎ 512 6853-12
- 🕐 Church daily 9:30–noon, 2–4. Crypt daily 9:30–4
- 🚇 U1, U3 Stephansplatz
- 🚌 Hopper 3A
- ♿ None
- 🎫 Church free; crypt moderate

Deceased emperors' hearts are preserved in the Augustinian Church (➤ 37), their embalmed entrails in the catacombs of St. Stephen's (➤ 43), and their bodies here in the Capuchin Crypt, a shrine for pilgrims and loyalists.

The Capuchins and their church The Franciscan Capuchins came to Austria in the reign of Duke (later Emperor) Matthias (1612–1619), whose wife, Empress Anna, founded their monastery in 1618. The preacher Marco d'Aviano, friend and adviser to Emperor Leopold I, was Vienna's most celebrated Capuchin. Famously intrepid, he went into battle with the imperial forces against the Turkish army, which was besieging Vienna in 1683. He died in the city in 1699 and is buried in one of the church's side chapels.

Simplicity The building is in accord with the austere precepts of the Capuchins. Almost the only decoration is a tasteless 1936 fresco of St. Francis of Assisi and a cross on the facade. Inside is the Kaiserkapelle (Emperor Chapel), with wooden statues of emperors Matthias and Ferdinand II, III, and IV. The Chapel of the Cross has an altar by Lukas von Hildebrandt and a very moving *pietà* (Mary embracing the dead Christ), with weeping angels and women by Peter Strudel and Matthias Steinl (1717).

Habsburg resting place The first emperor and empress to be buried in the crypt were Matthias and his wife Anna. Since then 138 members of the Habsburg family have been interred here, along with Maria Theresa's governess. The simple copper coffin of Joseph II, which contrasts with the elaborate baroque tombs, is a reminder of its occupant's distaste for religious excess.

STEPHANSDOM

St. Stephen's Cathedral has been the spiritual focus of the Viennese people since the Middle Ages. The great South Tower is affectionately known as the Steffl ("Little Steve"). Its huge Pummerin bell rings in the New Year on Austrian radio and TV.

Ornamentation From the three preceding Romanesque churches on this site, only the Giant's Door and Heathen Towers (so called because a pagan shrine was supposed to have been here) have survived as part of the Gothic church. Note the striking yellow, green, and black chevrons of the tiled roof and a representation of the Habsburg double-headed eagle. Against the north wall is the pulpit marking the spot where Giovanni Capistrano (1386–1456) preached fiery sermons against the Turks. The cathedral is considered a symbol of endurance, having undergone numerous stages of repair due to the ravages of the Turks, the Napoleonic French, and the Allies. All the Federal States contributed to the cathedral's restoration after World War II.

Inside the cathedral Anton Pilgram's Gothic pulpit with portraits of the fathers of the church is near the entrance. In the north aisle is a self-portrait of Pilgram holding a square and compass. The Gothic vaulting in the Albertine Choir (1304–1340) is especially beautiful. Tobias Pock's 1647 baroque altar painting shows the martyrdom of St. Stephen. In the north apse is the exquisite Wiener Neustädter Altar (1447). In the south apse is the magnificent marble tomb of Friedrich III (1440–1493).

HIGHLIGHTS

- Pilgram's pulpit
- Tomb of Prince Eugene of Savoy, Kreuzkapelle
- Johann Pock statues of Saints Sebastian, Leopold, Florian, and Rochus
- Nicolas van Leyden tomb of Friedrich III
- *Man of Sorrows* crucifix

INFORMATION

- ✚ H6
- ✉ Stephansplatz 3
- ☎ 5155 23767
- 🕐 Daily 6AM–10PM
- Ⓤ U1, U3 Stephansplatz
- 🚌 Bus 1A
- ♿ Good
- 🎟 Cathedral free; tour of choir moderate
- ↔ Peterskirche (▶ 40)
- ❓ Separate tours of cathedral and catacombs

Nave and high altar, St. Stephen's

KARLSKIRCHE

St. Charles's Church is one of Europe's finest baroque buildings. The complicated symbolism in the two exotic columns at the front illustrates Habsburg secular power and spiritual legitimacy.

Origins In 1713 Vienna was hit by the last of many plagues; Emperor Charles VI vowed to dedicate a church to St. Charles Borromeo, who succored the people during the 1576 Milan plague. Begun in 1716, it is the masterpiece of Johann Bernhard Fischer von Erlach, who died in 1723 leaving his son, Joseph Emanuel, to complete it in 1739.

Paean in stone The two columns at the front, modeled on Trajan's Column in Rome, symbolize the Pillars of Hercules in the Mediterranean, a reference to the Spanish realm (by then lost) of the other Habsburg line. Their spiraling friezes show the life and virtues of Charles Borromeo (Steadfastness on the left, Courage on the right, mirroring the emperor's motto "*Constantia et fortitudine*"). The russet, gold, and white interior creates a feeling of harmonious tranquillity.

HISTORISCHES MUSEUM DER STADT WIEN

Although housed in a drab 1950s–style building, the Viennese History Museum is one of Europe's best city museums, and its well-displayed contents bring the Viennese palimpsest vividly to life.

Origins The city's first historical museum was founded in 1887 and occupied several rooms in the newly built City Hall. Many plans were made for a purpose-built museum building but the council gave the go-ahead only in 1953. The characterless design of the structure—its banality made all the more striking by its juxtaposition with the baroque architecture of St. Charles's Church next door—aroused considerable anger among Viennese patriots, although it had its defenders.

Museum collection Vienna's history, topography, art, and culture are explored in the many works of art and architectural relics, and in the early city plans, reconstructions of interiors like Adolf Loos' living room and Franz Grillparzer's Biedermeier apartment, and beautifully made period models of the city.

Sweeping view The first floor spans prehistory (Hallstatt culture) up to and including medieval times. On the second floor are exhibits of the baroque period and Enlightenment. The material relating to the time of the Turkish siege of Vienna (weapons and a portrait of Turkish commander Kara Mustafa) is especially interesting. The third floor covers the Congress of Vienna (1814–1815), the Biedermeier era (1815–1848), the revolution of 1848, and Vienna at the beginning of the 20th century, with examples of the art, artifacts, and designs of the Vienna Secession (▶ 34), and the later Austrian Expressionism movement.

HIGHLIGHTS

- Edouard Fischer's maquette of old town, 1854
- Franz Xavier Messerschmidt's grotesque busts
- Augustin Hirschvogel's plan of Vienna, 1548
- *View of the Siege of Vienna* (1683), Franz Geffels
- Portrait of Kara Mustafa, the Turkish commander in 1683
- Johann Höchle's paintings of the final Napoleonic campaign
- *Stephansplatz* (1834), Rudolf von Alt
- Reconstructed apartment of playwright Franz Grillparzer
- Reconstructed sitting room in architect Adolf Loos' house
- *Anna Moll, Writing,* Carl Moll

INFORMATION

- H7
- Karlsplatz
- 505874 784021
- Tue–Sun 9–6
- Café
- U1, U2, U4 Karlsplatz
- Bus 4A; tram 62, 65
- Good
- Moderate
- Karlskirche (▶ 44)

SCHLOSS BELVEDERE

After St. Stephen's Cathedral (➤ 43), the restored Belvedere Palace is Vienna's most important landmark. It was built in the early 18th century for Prince Eugene of Savoy, the most successful general in Austria's history.

Schloss Belvedere, staircase

Origins Lukas von Hildebrandt constructed the Lower Belvedere (Unteres Belvedere) between 1714 and 1716. The magnificent Upper Belvedere (Oberes Belvedere), designed to house the prince's fabulous art collection, went up between 1721 and 1723.

The palace in history Emperor Josef II installed the Imperial Picture Gallery in the Upper Belvedere. Franz Ferdinand, the heir to the throne, lived here from 1894 until his assassination in 1914. In 1955 the Austrian State Treaty ending the Allied occupation was signed in the Marble Hall.

Museums The Lower Belvedere displays Austrian baroque art; the adjacent Orangery showcases medieval art. The Austrian Gallery in the Upper Belvedere contains 19th- and 20th-century paintings and sculpture, except for the Modern Gallery, which houses European works.

MUSEUM FÜR ANGEWANDTE KUNST

The refurbished Museum of Applied Art, the MAK, experiments with remarkable minimalist display techniques. A striking example is the projection of silhouettes of chairs against a white screen that emphasizes the abstract beauty of the individual designs.

Forerunner Established in 1864, and originally named the Museum of Art and Industry, this was the first museum of its kind in Europe. The initiative came from art historian Rudolf Eitelberger, who had been much impressed by London's South Kensington Museum, later the Victoria and Albert Museum.

Decorative The beautiful 1871 neo-Renaissance building by Heinrich Ferstel combines architecture with applied art—its facade is ornamented with impressive sgrafito and majolica portrait medallions of famous artist-craftsmen.

The interior Inside, a glass-enclosed entrance hall is surrounded by the arcades of higher storys. In the 1990s, an extension built between 1907 and 1909 was connected to the main part with a steel and glass passageway. On the north side is the University of Applied Arts.

The collections The amazingly rich collections include a fine selection of Jugendstil, Biedermeier, and Thonet furniture from Austria. There is a section devoted to artifacts from the East (textiles, carpets, ceramics), and another part contains European decorative art, including both Venetian and Bohemian glass, Meissen porcelain, and jewelry. The display of works by leading artists of the Wiener Werkstätte on the second floor alone is worth the visit.

HIGHLIGHTS

- Atrium (entrance hall), with Renaissance-style arcades
- 16th-century Egyptian silk carpet
- 15th-century Buddha head
- Intarsia table from Old University (1735)
- Meissen bear by J.G. Kirchner (1735)
- Bohemian glass
- Lobmeyr glass (Vienna)
- Biedermeier sofa with red covering (1830), by J. Danhauser
- Thonet bentwood furniture
- Furniture and artifacts by the Wiener Werkstätte

INFORMATION

- ✚ J6
- ✉ Stubenring 5
- ☎ Recorded information 112 8000
- 🕐 Tue 10–9, Wed–Sun 10–6. Closed May 1, Nov 1
- 🍴 Elegant café
- Ⓤ U3 Stubentor
- 🚃 Trams 1 and 2 on Ringstrasse
- Schnellbahn to Landstrasse
- Good
- Moderate
- ❓ Tours: audio-guide. Frequent special exhibitions, often avant-garde

47

HEERESGESCHICHTLICHES MUSEUM

HIGHLIGHTS

- Ornate Byzantine facade
- Life-size statues of Austria's greatest generals

Upper floor

- Montgolfier balloon
- *Portrait of Wallenstein*, J. Van Dyck
- Turkish tent
- *The Battle of Aspern*, J.P. Krafft

First floor

- "To the Unknown Soldier" (1916), Albin Egger Lienz
- Car in which Archduke Franz Ferdinand was assassinated
- Bloodstained uniform of Archduke Franz Ferdinand
- Tank park

INFORMATION

- J9
- Arsenal, Ghegastrasse Objekt 18
- 79 561-0
- Mon–Thu, Sat–Sun 9–5. Closed public hols
- Café
- Bus 13A to Südbahnhof; trams 0, D, 18 to Südbahnhof
- Schnellbahn to Südbahnhof
- Few
- Moderate
- Tours: audio-guide

The huge military complex known as the Arsenal and Museum of Military History is notable for its exotic pseudo–Byzantine architecture and for the collection inside, which provides a fascinating insight into Vienna's imperial history.

Riotproof After the revolution of 1848, during which the old town armory Am Hof was plundered, leading Ringstrassen architects were commissioned to design a riot-proof arms factory and depot. This state-of-the-art complex was built with eight fortress-like barracks along its perimeter; by 1854 the facilities it enclosed were like those of an entire city within a city. The task of constructing it created jobs at a time of social unrest and unemployment. After World War II, part of the complex was rebuilt, and part is now occupied by state-owned theater workshops and the central telephone exchange as well as the Museum of Military History.

Collection Themed sections include the Thirty Years War (1618–1648), the Napoleonic Wars, and the Austrian Navy (in existence until 1918). Particularly gruesome is the bloodstained tunic Archduke Franz Ferdinand, heir to the Habsburg throne, was assassinated in—this event triggered the start of World War I.

VIENNA's
best

CHURCHES

Anton Brückner

The composer Anton Brückner gave a recital on the organ in the Piaristenkirche in 1861 as part of his examination for a teaching post at the Music Conservatory. A long silence followed his second piece, during which the composer sat nervously with bowed head. The silence was broken by the senior examiner, who remarked in an awed whisper, "He should be examining us!"

Jesuitenkirche

ANNAKIRCHE

An intimate little gem of baroque architecture with Daniel Gran's ceiling fresco of the Immaculate Conception. In the side-chapel is a beautiful Gothic carving of Mary, Jesus, and St. Anne by Veit Stoss of Nürnberg.

✚ H6 ✉ Annagasse 3B ☎ 512 4797 ⏰ Daily 6AM–7PM Ⓜ U1, U3 to Stephansplatz

FRANZISKANERKIRCHE

Built next to a home for repentant prostitutes, whom Viennese burghers were encouraged to marry, this church later became the Franciscan monastery. The most notable feature is the illusionist architecture of Andrea Pozzo's high altar picture.

✚ H6 ✉ Franziskanerplatz 4 ☎ 512 4578
⏰ Mon–Sat 6AM–5:45PM; Sun 7AM–5:30PM Ⓜ U1, U3 to Stephansplatz

JESUITENKIRCHE

Andrea Pozzo designed the interior of this extremely ornate church in the early 18th century; it replaced a church built by the Jesuits soon after they had constructed the adjacent university, over which they gained control in 1622. From this base the Jesuits drove forward the Counter-Reformation in Vienna.

✚ H6 ✉ Dr-Ignaz-Seipel-Platz 1 ☎ 512 5232
⏰ Daily 7AM–6:30PM Ⓜ U3 to Stubentor

MARIA AM GESTADE

Danube boatmen once worshipped in this 14th-century Gothic church built on the former river bank (*Gestade*). The nave is not exactly aligned with the choir because the site was so small. The graceful spire, with its filigree decoration, is a landmark. The church was the center of a 19th-century religious revival by the Moravian preacher Clemens Maria Hofbauer, later patron saint of the city, whose tomb is here.

✚ H5/6 ✉ Salvatorgasse 12 ☎ 533 2282 ⏰ Daily (rear nave) 6:30AM–6PM. Access to choir on request Ⓜ U1, U4 to Schwedenplatz

MICHAELERKIRCHE

In the crypt of St. Michael's Church are mummified corpses in coffins, the lids of which have warped and lifted. Parts of this richly decorated building date to the late 13th century. Karl Georg Merville's dramatic stucco over the high altar depicts the fall of the angels, a theme continued in the sculpture by Lorenzo Mattielli over the portico.

📍 G6 ✉ Michaelerplatz 1 ☎ 533 8000 🕐 Daily 6:30AM–7PM 🚇 U3 to Herrengasse 🚌 Bus 2A to Michaelerplatz

PIARISTENKIRCHE
(MARIA TREU)

This lesser-known work by the great Lukas von Hildebrandt was built in 1716 for the Piarist teaching order. The marvelous rococo frescoes (1752–1753), depicting biblical scenes, are Vienna's finest example of the work of Franz Anton Maulbertsch.

📍 F6 ✉ Jodok-Fink-Platz–Piaristengasse 43 ☎ 406 1453-0 🕐 For mass or by appointment 🚌 Tram J to Theater in der Josefstadt

Ruprechtskirche

RUPRECHTSKIRCHE

St. Rupert's, Vienna's oldest surviving church built in the 11th century, was once patronized by salt merchants landing their wares on the Danube shore. A remaining portion of medieval stained glass in the choir shows the crucifixion, complemented by a vivid modern stained-glass window of the baptism of Christ.

📍 H6 ✉ Ruprechtsplatz ☎ 535 6003 🕐 Easter–Oct: Mon–Fri 10–1 🚇 U1, U4 to Schwedenplatz

VOTIVKIRCHE

This huge neo-Gothic church was built to commemorate Franz Josef's escape from an assassination attempt in 1853. Its chapels are dedicated to Austrian regiments. Note the Renaissance sarcophagus of Count Salm, defender of Vienna in the Turkish siege of 1529.

📍 G5 ✉ Rooseveltplatz 8 ☎ 406 1192-0 🕐 Daily 9–4 🚇 U2 🚌 Trams 1, 2 to Schottentor

WOTRUBA KIRCHE

This extraordinary modern church, designed by the sculptor Fritz Wotruba, seems to have been built with randomly jumbled concrete blocks and lit by arbitrarily placed narrow glass panels.

📍 Off map to southwest ✉ Georgsgasse/Rysergasse (Mauer, 13th District) ☎ 888 6147 🕐 Thu–Fri 2–4; Sat 2–8; Sun 9–5 🚌 Bus 60A; tram 60 from Hietzing-Mauerer Lange Gasse, then walk

Modern sanctuary

Fritz Wotruba went into exile in Switzerland before World War II and was one of the few of Austria's artistic and academic élite to return. He worked on his "Cyclopean church," now known as the Wotruba Kirche, for ten years starting in 1966, aiming to create sanctuary for meditation with modern materials. He died in 1976, a year before his very personal architectural statement was completed.

51

PALACES

See Top 25 Sights for
OBIZZI-PALACE (▶ 39)

KINSKY-PALAIS

One of Lukas von Hildebrandt's masterworks built in 1716, with a slim, elegant facade that overlooks the Freyung. Try to get a look at the ceremonial staircase inside and also its ceiling fresco, *Apotheosis of a War Hero*, which flatters Count Philipp von Daun, the military commander who first owned the palace.
➕ G6 ✉ Freyung 4 ⓘ Not normally accessible to the public 🚇 U2 to Schottentor 🚊 Trams 1, 2

Austrian Theater Museum

This is in the Lobkowitz Palace and gives an overview of drama in Austria from the 19th century onwards. Models of opera stage-sets designed by the Secession artist Alfred Roller are on view; he helped Gustav Mahler revolutionize opera production. The loveliest room is the Eroica-Saal where Beethoven first conducted and played several of his works.

LOBKOWITZ-PALAIS

This noble palace was built between 1685 and 1687 by Giovanni Tencala for the powerful Dietrichstein family, but the present impressive facade is by Johann Bernhard Fischer von Erlach. After the Lobkowitzes acquired it in 1753, it became the center for social and artistic life; Beethoven's Eroica Symphony was given its first performance here in 1804, and during the Congress of Vienna many famous balls were held. "The congress dances, but it doesn't progress," quipped Prince de Ligne. The Austrian Theater Museum is now here.
➕ H6 ✉ Lobkowitzplatz 2 ☎ 512 8800 ⓘ Tue–Sun 10–5; Wed 10–9pm 🚇 U1, U2, U4 to Karlsplatz/Oper ⓘ Moderate

SCHÖNBORN-BATTHYÁNY PALAIS

The Hungarian Bán (Governor) of Croatia, Adam Batthyány, commissioned Johann Bernhard Fischer von Erlach's most impressive palace, built in 1698. The long monumental facade is enlivened with reliefs of a triumphal procession in antiquity and with allegories of wisdom and fame. Reliefs above the side-window show Hercules taming the Bull of Minos and scenes from Roman mythology.
➕ G6 ✉ Renngasse 4 ⓘ Not accessible to the public 🚇 U2 🚊 Trams 1, 2 to Schottentor

Grand entrance of the Schönborn-Batthyány Palais

SCHWARZENBERG-PALAIS

In 1716, Prince Schwarzenberg bought an unfinished palace by Lukas von Hildebrandt and then commissioned Johann Bernhard Fischer von Erlach, and later his son Josef Emanuel, to complete what is now one of Vienna's best hotels (▶ 84); it is still owned by the family. The grand sweep up to the portico was conceived by the younger Fischer, who

The front of the Kinsky-Palais

also installed Vienna's first steam-driven motor to pump water for the fountains. The Schwarzenbergs' neighbor and rival, Prince Eugene of Savoy, had to postpone his great Belvedere project (▶ 46) until he had persuaded them to sell a vital piece of adjacent land.

🔒 H7 ✉ Schwarzenbergplatz 9 ☎ Hotel/restaurant: 798 4515 🚊 Tram D to Schwarzenbergplatz

TRAUTSON-PALAIS

Smaller yet elegant, this is another palace designed by Fischer von Erlach the elder, built in 1710, and was the headquarters of Maria Theresa's Hungarian Lifeguards. It is now the Ministry of Justice.

🔒 G6 ✉ Museumstrasse 7 🕓 Not accessible to the public 🚇 U2, U3 to the Volkstheater

PRINZ-EUGEN-WINTERPALAIS

The two greatest architects of their age—Johann Bernhard Fischer von Erlach and Lukas von Hildebrandt—both worked on the Winter Palace of Eugene (1695–1698), although the former was careful to claim the credit for it. You can see the fabulous ceremonial stairway and, during special exhibitions, the frescoes of Apollo and Hercules, symbolizing Prince Eugene of Savoy's many talents.

🔒 H6 ✉ Himmelpfortgasse 8 ☎ 51 433 🕓 Vestibule: Mon–Thu 8–4; Fri 8–3:30 🚇 U1, U3 to Stephansplatz 💵 Free

WITTGENSTEIN HAUS

Ludwig Wittgenstein, one of the most famous philosophers of the 20th century, designed this austere house for his sister in the 1920s. The house reflects its creator's intellect; built in the Bauhaus style, it is curious rather than architecturally appealing.

🔒 K6 ✉ Parkgasse 18 ☎ 713 7495 🕓 Mon–Fri 9–noon, 2–6 🚇 U3 to Rochusgasse 💵 Free ❓ Accessible for functions of the Bulgarian Cultural Institute

Schwarzenberg family

The influential Schwarzenbergs had vast estates in Bohemia and palaces in Austria. They supplied the Habsburgs with senior clerics, generals, politicians, and administrators. The current Prince Schwarzenberg is said to have ironically thanked Queen Elizabeth II for "bombing his palace into a hotel"—hotel-keeping paid for restoring his mansion after the war. After the 1989 "Velvet Revolution" in Prague he acted as adviser to the Czech President Václav Havel.

MUSEUMS & GALLERIES

In the Sigmund Freud Museum

Duke Rudolf IV

The likeness of Rudolf IV (1339–1365) in the Cathedral Museum, painted in his last year by a Bohemian master, is claimed as the first individual royal portrait in the German territories. Rudolf, called "the Founder," started the South Tower of the Stephansdom and founded the University of Vienna in 1364. He also forged documents tracing his line back to Julius Caesar, and awarded himself several impressive titles.

ALBERTINA
Louis Montoyer built this gallery between 1801 and 1804 to house the magnificent collection of drawings, engravings, and watercolors assembled by Duke Albert of Sachsen-Teschen.
➕ H6 ✉ Augustinerstrasse 1 (exhibitions at Makartgasse 3 during closure) ☎ 53 483-0 🕐 Telephone for information about reopening after refurbishment 🚇 U1, U2, U4 to Karlsplatz/Oper 💷 Moderate

BESTATTUNGSMUSEUM
In this Burial Museum, devoted to the undertaker's art, exhibits include photographs of dressed corpses seated on chairs, a stiletto for stabbing the dead through the heart to ensure against being buried alive, and a coffin bell-pull for use in such an emergency.
➕ H8 ✉ Goldeggasse 19 ☎ 5019 54227 🕐 By appointment Mon–Fri noon–3PM 🚋 Tram D to Upper Belvedere 💷 Moderate

DOM UND DIÖZESANMUSEUM
The Cathedral Museum's most celebrated item is a portrait of Duke Rudolf IV, but there are also fine medieval woodcarvings and paintings by masters such as Lukas Cranach and Franz Anton Maulbertsch.
➕ H6 ✉ Stephansplatz 6, Stiege 1/1 ☎ 5155 23560 or 5155 23689 🕐 Tue–Sat 10–5 🚇 U1, U3 to Stephansplatz 💷 Moderate

JEWISH MUSEUM
Here you'll find thought-provoking exhibitions of Judaica. On the Judenplatz is Rachel Whitehead's famous Holocaust Memorial.
➕ H6 ✉ Dorotheergasse 11 ☎ 535 0431 🕐 Sun–Fri 10–6; Thu 10–8 🚇 U1, U3 to Stephansplatz 💷 Moderate

IMPERIAL FUNITURE DEPOT
Fascinating panorama of furniture made by craftsmen patronized by the Habsburg from the time of Maria Theresa onwards.
➕ F7 ✉ Mariahilfer Strasse 88 ☎ 524 3357 🕐 Daily 9–5 🚇 U3 to Neubaugasse 💷 Moderate

LIPIZZANER MUSEUM WIEN

Photographs, antique tack, uniforms, and videos and displays on the training of the Lipizzaners, plus a peek at the horses in their stalls.

🔢 G6 ⊠ Stallburg/Hofburg Reitschulgasse 2 ☎ 533 7811 🕐 Daily 9–6. Tours by arrangement 🚇 U3 to Herrengasse 🎫 Moderate

TECHNISCHES MUSEUM

Here you can explore the inventions and technical development of Austria from earliest times.

🔢 D8 ⊠ Mariahilfer Strasse 212 ☎ 914 1610 🕐 Mon–Sat 9–6, Sun 10–6 (late opening Thu 8pm) 🚋 Tram 52, 58 🎫 Moderate

SECULAR AND SACRED TREASURIES
(SCHATZKAMMER: HOFBURG, ► 35)

The insignia and crown (AD 962) of the Holy Roman Emperor, a mid-15th-century Burgundian goblet, the Imperial Cross (c1024), and the so-called "Sword of Charlemagne" (late 9th century) are the stars here.

🔢 G6 ⊠ Schweizerhof (Hofburg) ☎ 533 6046 🕐 Mon–Wed 10–6 🚇 U3 to Herrengasse 🚌 Hopper 2A to Michaelerplatz 🎫 Moderate

WIENER STRASSENBAHNMUSEUM

You can join a round trip on a vintage tram and visit the Tramway Museum starting from Karlsplatz.

🔢 L8 ⊠ Erdbergstrasse 109 ☎ 7909 44903 🕐 May–Oct: Sat–Sun 9–4 🚇 U3 to Erdberg, then a short walk 🎫 Inexpensive

MUSEUM QUARTER

Relocated to this long-awaited quarter occupying the former imperial stables, with a late-2001 debut, are the Museum of Modern Art (formerly in the Liechtenstein Palace) and the Kunsthalle (currently holding shows of contemporary art in Karlsplatz). The new Leopold Collection, also here, houses the finest assemblage of works by Gustav Klimt, Egon Schiele, and other artists of the period.

🔢 G7 ⊠ Messepalast

Reforming emperor

Emperor Joseph II sometimes carried rationalism to extremes—as when he decreed that coffins be reusable, with exit flaps for the corpses. However, he founded both the General Hospital, with its revolutionary "Fool's Tower" (► 26), and the Josephinum (► 27). The Vienna Medical School, founded under Maria Theresa, subsequently became world famous, especially for its introduction of new diagnostic techniques.

The grandeur of the Heeresgeschichtliches Museum

PARKS & GARDENS

Ferris wheel on the

The big wheel

The giant Ferris wheel on the Prater, built in 1896 by Englishman Walter Basset, was where Harry Lime met his old friend in the movie *The Third Man*. The wheel rotates at about 30 inches per second and offers great views.

🕐 Feb 19–Apr 30, Oct 1–Nov 13: daily 10AM–10PM. May 1–Sep 30: daily 9:30AM–11PM. Dec 26–Jan 8: daily 11AM–8PM

**See Top 25 Sights for
SCHÖNBRUNN PARK (➤ 25)**

AUGARTEN

Joseph II opened these gardens to the public in 1775 (much to the irritation of the upper classes, who had walked in them by invitation).
✚ H4 ⊠ Obere Augartenstrasse 1 ☎ Porcelain Museum 21 124-11 🕐 Porcelain Museum Mon–Fri 9:30–6. Park daily 6AM–dusk 🚊 Tram N from Schwedenplatz 🎟 Inexpensive (tours of museum)

BURGGARTEN

The vast Jugendstil glasshouse built by Friedrich Ohmann in 1907 replaced the earliest glass and iron structure in Vienna (1826).
✚ G6/7 ⊠ Burgring/Opernring 🕐 Apr–Sep: daily 6AM–10PM. Oct–Mar: daily 6AM–8PM 🚊 Trams 1, 2 to Burgring

PRATER

The former imperial hunting grounds were opened to the public in 1766, and now include a chestnut avenue, a fairground, and other leisure facilities.
✚ K5–N8 ⊠ Praterstern 🕐 Funfair: Mar–Oct: daily 8AM–midnight 🚇 U1 to Praterstern 🚊 Tram 0 🎟 Moderate (all attractions)

STADTPARK

Laid out in 1863 on the old River Wien causeway, the park is packed with monuments to the composers and artists of 19th-century Vienna (➤ 57).
✚ H/J6/7 ⊠ Stubenring 🕐 Daily 8AM–dusk 🚇 U3 to Stubentor, U4 to Stadtpark 🚊 Trams 1, 2

VOLKSGARTEN

Dominated by the Doric Theseus-Tempel, Volksgarten is an oasis of tranquillity in the heart of the city.
✚ G6 ⊠ Dr-Karl-Renner-Ring 🕐 May–Sep: daily 6AM–10PM. Oct–Apr: daily 6AM–9PM 🚇 U3 to Volkstheater 🚊 Trams 1, 2

Relaxing in the Burggarten

STATUES & MONUMENTS

DONNER FOUNTAIN
This is a copy of Georg Raphael Donner's *Providentia Fountain*, which is in the Baroque Museum of the Belvedere (► 46). Maria Theresa disapproved of the nude figures. The water nymphs symbolize the rivers that form the borders of Lower Austria.
➕ H6 ✉ Neuer Markt 🚇 U1, U3 to Stephansplatz

HENRY MOORE SCULPTURE
Henry Moore gave his *Hill Arches* sculpture to the city in 1978 on the condition that it was sited on the Karlsplatz.
➕ H7 ✉ Karlsplatz 🚇 U1, U2, U4 to Karlsplatz

JOHANN STRAUSS MONUMENT
The favorite statue of the Viennese Waltz King represents him with unrestrained, and gilded, sentimentality.
➕ H7 ✉ Stadtpark 🚋 Trams 1, 2 to Weihburggasse

LUEGER MONUMENT
Austria's most famous mayor (1897–1910) was also notoriously anti-Semitic.
➕ H6 ✉ Dr-Karl-Lueger-Platz 🚇 U3 to Stubentor

MONUMENT TO EMPRESS ELISABETH
Erected following the assassination of the popular empress by an anarchist in Geneva in 1898.
➕ G6 ✉ Volksgarten (Burgtheater end) 🚋 Trams 1, 2 to Burgtheater

MONUMENT TO FRANZ-JOSEPH
Austria's penultimate and longest-reigning monarch (1848–1916) is shown in his military uniform, to which he had a sentimental attachment.
➕ G6 ✉ Burggarten 🚋 Trams 1, 2 to Burgring

MONUMENT TO MARIA THERESA
The great reforming empress (1740–1780) is shown enthroned and surrounded by her generals and ministers.
➕ G6 ✉ Burgring 🚋 Trams 1, 2 to Burgring

MONUMENT TO THE VICTIMS OF FASCISM
Directly opposite the Albertina stands Austrian sculptor Alfred Hrdlickla's moving memorial to those tortured and killed in the Gestapo headquarters (Hotel Metropole) that stood here.
➕ H6 ✉ Morzinplatz 🚇 U1, U4 to Schwedenplatz

MOZART MONUMENT
Austria's greatest composer is portrayed as 19th-century people liked to imagine him.
➕ G6 ✉ Burggarten 🚋 Trams 1, 2 to Burgring

Strauss monument in the Stadtpark

War memorial
The Viennese, who had been treated horrifically by the Russian liberation army in 1945, were not pleased by the heroically represented figure in the middle of the Russian Liberation Monument in the Schwarzenbergplatz—officially it is "The Unknown Soldier." More appropriate names for it were immediately found, typically "The Unknown Plunderer" or "The Unknown Rapist."

JUGENDSTIL & SECESSION

Jugendstil

In German-speaking lands, art nouveau was known as Jugendstil (youth style). Vienna developed its own closely related style, Secession—so called because its proponent artists "seceded" from the conservative Association of Fine Artists in 1897 (➤ 34). Josef Hoffman was one of the leaders.

Secession style at Karlsplatz station

**See Top 25 Sights for
KIRCHE AM STEINHOF (➤ 24)**

ANKERUHR
Every hour, a single figure from Austrian history revolves across the face of the Anchor Clock; they all appear daily at noon.
➕ H6 ✉ Hoher Markt 10–11 🚇 U1, U4 to Schwedenplatz

ARTARIA HAUS
Max Fabiani's Artaria House is one of the most striking Jugendstil buildings in the city.
➕ H6 ✉ Kohlmarkt 9 🚇 U3 to Herrengasse

ÖSTERREICHISCHES POSTSPARKASSENAMT
The functionalism of the Austrian Post Office Savings Bank (built 1910–1912) made it seem far in advance of its time.
➕ J6 ✉ Georg-Coch-Platz ☎ 51 400 🕐 Mon, Wed, Fri 8–3; Thu 8–5:30 🚇 U1, U4 to Schwedenplatz

JOSEF HOFFMANN VILLA COLONY ON THE HOHE WARTE
It is worth the 20-minute tram ride to see these elegant villas.
➕ G1 ✉ Steinfeldgasse/Wollergasse 🚋 Tram 37 to last stop

KARLSPLATZ PAVILIONS
Otto Wagner, the great Secession architect, designed the City Transit Railway. The finest stations are the two on Karlsplatz (1898) and the emperor's own at Schönbrunn.
➕ H7 ✉ Karlsplatz ☎ 505 8747-84059 🕐 Tue–Sun 9–noon. Closed Nov 1–Mar 31 🚇 U1, U2, U4 to Karlsplatz

LOOS HAUS
Adolf Loos designed this building for a fashionable tailor. It is now a bank with an exhibition area. Because of its plain facade it was known as the "house without eyebrows," but it is luxurious inside.
➕ G6
✉ Michaelerplatz 3
☎ 21 136-2114
🕐 Mon, Tue, Wed, Fri 8–3; Thu 8–5:30
🚇 U3 to Herrengasse
🚌 Hopper 2A to Michaelerplatz

COFFEE HOUSES

BRÄUNERHOF
An old-fashioned café, with famously cantankerous waiters, this place is very pleasant, and there is a wide choice of newspapers.

🚩 H6 ✉ Stallburggasse 2 ☎ 512 3893 🕐 Mon–Fri 7:30AM–8:30PM; Sat 7:30AM–7PM; Sun 10AM–7PM 🚌 Hopper 2A to Habsburgergasse

CAFÉ MUSEUM
The original, spartan design was by Adolf Loos; today's minimalist furnishings still justify the nickname Café Nihilismus.

🚩 G7 ✉ Friedrichstrasse 6 ☎ 586 5202 🕐 Daily 8AM–midnight 🚇 U1, U2, U4 to Karlsplatz/Oper

CAFÉ CENTRAL
The lifelike figure seated near the entrance is Peter Altenberg, wittiest chronicler of early 20th-century Viennese life, and a regular patron.

🚩 G6 ✉ Herrengasse 14 ☎ 5333 76326 🕐 Mon–Sat 8AM–10PM. Closed Sun 🚇 U3 to Herrengasse

DEMEL
A confectioner with an imperial tradition, and a must on every tourist's itinerary (▶ 67).

🚩 G6 ✉ Kohlmarkt 14 ☎ 535 1717-39 🕐 Daily 9:30–7 🚇 U3 to Herrengasse

HAWELKA
Bohemians, literati, and night-owls frequent Leopold Hawelka's cramped café.

🚩 H6 ✉ Dorotheergasse 6 ☎ 512 8230 🕐 Mon, Wed–Sat 8AM–2AM; Sun 4PM–2AM. Closed Tue 🚇 U1, U3 to Stephansplatz

LANDTMANN
An elegant Ringstrassen café with a cellar where there's fringe theater and a pleasant summer terrace.

🚩 G6 ✉ Dr-Karl-Lueger-Ring 4 ☎ 532 0621 🕐 Daily 8AM–midnight 🚌 Trams 1, 2 to Burgtheater/Rathaus

Wax model of Peter Altenberg in the Café Central

Coffee and cakes

Coffee houses flourished in early 20th-century Vienna, when writers and artists used them for discussion, and as workplaces, unofficial banks, and mailboxes. A few that retain the traditional atmosphere are listed here. All serve a bewildering range of coffees. Freshly baked apfelstrudel is a typical accompaniment, and most places offer a simple menu of hot dishes.

The famous Café Demel

59

WHAT'S UP FOR KIDS

MÄRCHENBÜHNE "DER APFELBAUM"

Fairy tales are enacted with puppets at the Apple-Theatre for Fairy Tales. Periodic performances are given in English (check by phone).

✚ F7 ✉ Kirchengasse 41 ☎ 5231 72920 🕐 Performances Sat 3, 4:30 (irregularly at other times as well) 🚇 U3 to Neubaugasse ✋ Moderate

HAUS DES MEERES

The House of the Sea aquarium is in a World War II bomb shelter. There's plenty for young visitors to shudder at, including piranhas and sharks.

✚ F7 ✉ Esterhazypark ☎ 587 1417 🕐 Daily 9–6 🚇 U3 to Neubaugasse ✋ Moderate

KINDERFREIBAD, AUGARTEN

If your youngsters are ages 6 to 15, you can leave them in the supervised swimming pool here while you see the Augarten (▶ 56).

✚ H4 ✉ Augarten, Karl-Meissl-Gasse entrance ☎ 332 4258 🕐 Mon–Fri 10–6 🚌 Bus 5a from Nestroyplatz 🚋 Tram 5 to Wallensteinplatz ✋ Free

Prater in the dark

PRATER

This world-famous amusement park has many diversions; the Ferris wheel (the Reisenrad) is among the most popular.

✚ K5 ✉ Praterstern 🕐 Mar–Oct: 8AM–midnight 🚇 U1 to Praterstern 🚋 Tram 0

SAFARI PARK, GÄNSERNDORF

The park has 650 species and an adventure park where kids can stroke baby animals.

✚ Off map, 18 miles to northeast ✉ Siebenbrunnerstrasse, Gänserndorf ☎ 02282 702610 🕐 Mon–Fri 9:30–dusk or 4:30PM; Sat–Sun 9–dusk or 5:30PM 🚇 Schnellbahn from Wien Mitte ✋ Expensive ❓ Accessible by car (B8) via Deutsch Wagram

Fun for the young

Kids can have fun just getting around Vienna on the horse-drawn fiacres (cabs) and on the tram. The more exotic and impressive sights on the adult itinerary (such as the Hofburg and Schönbrunn) are also bound to please.

WIENER EISLAUFVEREIN

You could combine a visit to the Vienna Ice-skating Club (▶ 78) with lunch at the Hotel Inter-Continental Wien (▶ 62, 84).

✚ H7 ✉ Lothringerstrasse 22 ☎ 713 6353-0 🕐 Oct–Mar: Sat–Mon 9–8; Tue, Thu, Fri 9–9; Wed 9–10 🚇 U4 to Stadtpark ✋ Moderate ❓ Disco Tue, Fri

ZOO (TIERGARTEN) IN SCHÖNBRUNN

The former imperial menagerie is now Vienna's zoo.

✚ C9 ✉ Schönbrunn Park ☎ 877 9294 🕐 Summer: daily 9–6:30. Winter: daily 9AM–dusk 🚇 U4 to Schönbrunn ✋ Moderate

VIENNA
where to...

BEST IN TOWN

Prices

Expect to pay per person for a meal, excluding drink:

$$$	=	AS900–1,400; 65–101 euros
$$	=	AS500–900; 36–65 euros
$	=	AS150–500; 11–36 euros

Neue Wiener Küche

Nouvelle cuisine arrived late in the city. The man chiefly responsible for its introduction was Werner Matt, a Tyrolean chef who came to the Hilton in the 1970s. As a result, *Selbstmord mit Gabel und Messer* (suicide with a knife and fork) subsided. Menus grew shorter, and the city's kitchens began to use more fresh produce to reduce flour, fat, and deep-frozen ingredients.

ALTWIENERHOF ($$$)

Serious food lovers brave the gloom of the region near the Westbahnhof to sample chef Rudi Kellner's French cooking. The menu ranges over game and fish, and there's a large selection of French cheeses. The choice of French wines is the best in the city.

🔲 E8 ✉ Herklotzgasse 6 ☎ 892 6000 🕐 Mon–Fri noon–2, 6:30–11; Sat 6:30–11 🚇 U3 to Westbahnhof

DO & CO. IM HAAS-HAUS ($$$)

An extremely fashionable restaurant on the top floor of the Haas-Haus (► 16), with views of Stephansdom. Shellfish is a specialty, and there are also *teppanyaki* and Thai dishes.

🔲 H6 ✉ 7th floor, Haas-Haus, Stephansplatz 12 ☎ 535 3969 🕐 Daily noon–3, 6PM–midnight 🚇 U1, U3 to Stephansplatz

HEITZINGER BRÄU ($$$)

If you want to sample the famous *Wiener Tafelspitz* (boiled beef) at its most luxurious, as well as other beef specialties, this is the place. The atmosphere is ultra-Viennese and the restaurant is in the gracious suburb of Hietzing, close to Schönbrunn.

🔲 B8 ✉ Auhofstrasse 1 ☎ 877 7087 🕐 Daily 11:30–3, 6–10:30 🚇 U4 to Hietzing 🚋 Trams 58, 52, 10 to Kennedy Brücke

IM PALAIS SCHWARZENBERG ($$$)

The view of the gardens of the palace is splendid. So is the food. Try the stuffed guinea fowl in white port sauce or the medallions of venison.

🔲 H7 ✉ Schwarzenbergplatz 9 ☎ 798 4515/600 🕐 Daily noon–3, 6–11 🚋 Trams D, 1, 2 to Schwarzenbergplatz

KORSO BEI DER OPER ($$$)

Many consider this elegant restaurant in the Hotel Bristol the best in town, with the finest Viennese cuisine.

🔲 H7 ✉ Mahlerstrasse 2 ☎ 5151 6546 🕐 Sun–Fri noon–3PM, 6PM–1AM. Closed Sun lunch Jul 🚇 U1, U2, U4 to Oper

STEIRERECK ($$$)

This distinguished restaurant in Vienna's diplomatic quarter is famous for the delicacy of its *Neue Wiener Küche* and its well-chosen wine list.

🔲 J7 ✉ Rasumofskygasse 2 ☎ 713 3168 🕐 Mon–Fri 11:30–2:30 🚇 U3 to Rochusgasse

VIER JAHRESZEITEN ($$$)

Inventive cuisine from master chef Manfred Buchinger makes this one of the most interesting of Vienna's restaurants. The crustaceans are excellent, and the wines serious.

🔲 H7 ✉ Hotel Inter-Continental Wien, Johannesgasse 28 ☎ 7112 2143 🕐 Mon–Fri noon–3, 7–11 🚇 U4 to Stadtpark

OTHER VIENNESE RESTAURANTS

BEI MAX ($$)

Carinthian noodles are a specialty at this haunt of actors and writers; other regional dishes available.

🟦 G6 ✉ Landhausgasse 2, corner of Herrengasse ☎ 533 7359 🕐 Mon–Fri 11–11 🚇 U3 to Herrengasse

DREI HUSAREN ($$$)

A taste of the old Austro-Hungarian monarchy in gracious surroundings, with luxurious table settings and courteous service.

🟦 H6 ✉ Weihburggasse 4 ☎ 512 1092 🕐 Daily noon–3, 6–1 🚇 U1, U3 to Stephansplatz

ECKEL ($$$)

A charming restaurant in a series of *Stüberln* (annexes), offering recipes from grandfather Eckel's legendary cookbook. Superb service.

🟦 F2 ✉ Sieveringer Strasse 46 ☎ 320 3218 🕐 Tue–Sat noon–2:30, 6–10:30 🚇 U6 🚋 39A from Nussdorfer Strasse

FIGLMÜLLER ($$)

Always crowded, but good value, with huge schnitzels and a choice of wines by the glass. No beer.

🟦 H6 ✉ Wollzeile 5 ☎ 512 6177 🕐 Daily 11–10PM 🚇 U1, U3 to Stephansplatz

OSWALD UND KALB ($$)

Favored haunt of media glitterati, partly because it is open late. The specialty wine is Styrian Schilcher, made from indigenous grapes.

🟦 H6 ✉ Bäckerstrasse 14 ☎ 512 1371 🕐 Daily 6PM–2AM 🚇 U3 to Stubentor

WRENKH ($$$)

Exquisite vegetarian cuisine like wild rice risotto with mushrooms, and Greek fried rice with vegetables, sheep's cheese, and olives.

🟦 H6 ✉ Bauernmarkt 10 ☎ 533 1526 🕐 Daily 11AM–11:30PM 🚇 U1, U3 to Stephansplatz

ZU DEN 3 HACKEN ($$)

Good service and a noisy, convivial atmosphere. Some of the cooking has a Styrian flavor.

🟦 H6 ✉ Singerstrasse 28 ☎ 512 5895 🕐 Mon–Sat 9–midnight 🚇 U1, U3 to Stephansplatz

ZUM HERKNER ($$)

Excellent Viennese food carrying on the tradition of the restaurant's celebrated late owner.

🟦 B3 ✉ Dornbacher Strasse 123 ☎ 485 4386 🕐 Mon–Fri noon–2, 6–9:30 🚋 Tram 43 from Schottentor to last stop

ZUM SCHWARZEN KAMEEL ($$–$$$)

For a charming, extremely Viennese lunch, try the Jugendstil Black Camel, where you can munch on delicately prepared sandwiches.

🟦 H6 ✉ Bognergasse 5 (parallel to Naglergasse) ☎ 533 8125 🕐 Mon–Sat noon–2:30, 6–10:30 🚇 U1, U3 to Stephansplatz

ZUR TABAKSPFEIFE ($$)

Intimate, reliable, and unpretentious. Try the calf's liver or veal cutlet.

🟦 H6 ✉ Goldschmiedgasse 4 ☎ 533 7286 🕐 Mon–Fri 11AM–11PM; Sat 11AM–3PM 🚇 U1, U3 to Stephansplatz

The *Beisl*

Most restaurants that offer genuine Viennese cooking are carrying on the *Beisl* tradition: honest food, cooked and served in unpretentious surroundings. The word is of Yiddish origin (in the past, tavern keepers were often Jewish). Prosperity, tourism, and the profit motive have transformed some *Beisls* into expensive restaurants, but many hold to tradition and keep prices fair. Typical dishes include *Tafelspitz* (boiled beef), *Zwiebelrostbraten* (beefsteak with crispy onions), and *Beuschel* (chopped lung in sauce). Liver is also popular.

HEURIGEN

Heurigen

A *Heurigen* is a tavern in its own vineyard in the Wienerwald (Viennese Woods), traditionally selling only the current year's (*heuer*) wine. A selection of *Heurigen* from four different villages in the northern suburbs (approximately 6–7 miles from the Ringstrasse) are given here. Heiligenstadt is the village where Beethoven lived at the time he was going deaf, and his lodgings at Probusgasse 6 are now a museum. When open, a *Heurigen* is *ausg'steckt*, indicated by a bunch of fir-twigs hung outside the door. The basic wine is *Gemischter Satz*, a tindery white blend of local grapes. Roast meats, cheeses, and salads are served in most *Heurigen*, although some in Grinzing and Heiligenstadt are full-scale restaurants. The atmosphere is quintessentially Viennese—nostalgic, even maudlin after everyone has had a few glasses. Above all it's *gemütlich* (cozy), with *Schrammelmusik* (named after the 19th-century Schrammel brothers) played on fiddle, guitar, and accordion.

GRINZING

BACH-HENGL ($$)

This is a typical, family-run *Heurigen* in the heart of the tourist district, with garden tables in summer, Schrammel music, hot and cold buffets, and *Gemischter Satz* to drink.

✚ F1 ✉ Sandgasse 7–9 ☎ 320 2439 ⏰ 4PM–midnight 🚊 Tram 38 from Schottentor to end stop

REINPRECHT ($–$$)

A 300-year-old former monastery.

✚ F1 ✉ Cobenzlgasse 22 ☎ 320 1471 ⏰ 3:30PM–midnight 🚊 Tram 38 to last stop, then a short walk

HEILIGENSTADT

FEUERWEHR-WAGNER ($$)

Pleasant, intimate, and rustic establishment that is very popular in winter.

✚ F1 ✉ Grinzingerstrasse 53 ☎ 320 2442 ⏰ 4PM–midnight 🚇 U4, U6 🚌 Bus 38A from Heiligenstadt Station

MAYER AM PFARRPLATZ ($$)

One of the best *Heurigen* in Heiligenstadt. There are several rooms and a large garden.

✚ G1 ✉ Heiligenstädter Pfarrplatz 2 ⏰ 4PM–midnight 🚇 U4, U6 🚌 Bus 38A from Heiligenstadt Station

ZIMMERMANN ($$)

An oasis off the beaten track near the Beethoven House where the composer's tragic *Heiligenstädter Testament* was written in 1802.

✚ G1 ✉ Armbrustergasse 5 ☎ 370 2211 ⏰ Mon–Sat 5PM–midnight 🚇 U4, U6 🚌 Bus 38A from Heiligenstadt Station

NEUSTIFT AM WALDE

FUHRGASSL-HUBER ($$)

One of the most congenial taverns in the village's long main street. The same family also runs an excellent pension close by (▶ 86).

✚ C1 ✉ Neustift am Walde 68 ☎ 440 1405 ⏰ 2PM–midnight 🚇 U6 🚌 Bus 35A from Nussdorfer Strasse

STAMMERSDORF

FEITZINGER ($)

In an area seldom visited by tourists, this tavern has pleasant rustic interiors and serves an excellent house wine.

✚ Off map to northeast ✉ Stammersdorfer Strasse 115 ☎ 292 9642 ⏰ Mar–Nov: Mon–Sun 1PM–midnight. Closed Wed 🚊 Tram 31 from Schottenring to last stop

URBAN ($)

Small and intimate, with a charming garden and fountain.

✚ Off map to northeast ✉ Stammersdorfer Strasse 123 ☎ 292 6154 ⏰ Oct–Apr: Sat–Sun, hols 2–10. May–Sep: daily 🚊 Tram 31 from Schottenring to last stop

QUICK BITES

AUGUSTINER-KELLER ($$)

Good Austrian and Viennese food, plus local wines. A bit touristy.

H6 ✉ Augustinerstrasse 1 ☎ 533 1026 🕐 Daily 11–midnight 🚇 U1, U2, U4 to Oper

ESTERHAZYKELLER ($)

The Esterhazys gave free wine to the populace here during the 1683 Turkish siege. The wine is no longer free but it's still very good value. Simple food.

G6 ✉ Haarhof 1 (off Wallnerstrasse) ☎ 533 3482 🕐 Mon–Fri 11–10; Sat–Sun 4–10 🚇 U3 to Herrengasse

MELKER STIFTSKELLER ($)

An echoing baroque cellar that serves very acceptable food.

G6 ✉ Schottengasse 3 ☎ 533 5530 🕐 Tue–Sat 5PM–midnight 🚇 U2 to Schottentor

NASCHMARKT ($)

This first-rate self-service chain serves Austrian food in agreeable surroundings with comfortable seating.

G6 ✉ Schottengasse 1 ☎ 533 5186 🕐 Mon–Fri 10:30–9; Sat–Sun, hols 10:30–3 🚇 U2 to Schottentor
Also at:
H7 ✉ Schwarzenbergplatz 16 ☎ 505 3115 🕐 Mon–Fri 6:30AM–10:30PM; Sat–Sun, hols 9AM–10:30PM 🚋 Trams 1,2, D to Schwarzenbergplatz

NORDSEE ($–$$)

Not just fish and chips. You'll find a wide range of seafood dishes and sandwiches with fish fillings. Self-service.

H6 ✉ Kohlmarkt 6 ☎ 533 5966 🕐 Mon–Fri 10AM–8PM; Sat–Sun 10AM–8PM 🚇 U1, U3 to Stephansdom
Also at:
Kärntner Strasse 25, Neubaugasse 9, Mariahilfer Strasse 84, and others

TRZESNIEWSKI ($)

Lots of open-face sandwiches, with toppings of fish, meat, vegetables, poultry, and eggs from free-range chickens.

H6 ✉ Dorotheergasse 1 ☎ 512 3291 🕐 Mon–Fri 8:30–7:30; Sat 9–5 🚇 U1, U3 to Stephansplatz
Also at:
Galleria, Landstrasse Hauptstrasse 97–101, Mariahilfer Strasse 95, Am Meiselmarkt, and others

ZWÖLF APOSTEL-KELLER ($)

A student hang-out. Very atmospheric cellars on three levels.

H6 ✉ Sonnenfelsgasse 3 ☎ 512 6777 🕐 4:30PM–midnight 🚇 U1, U3 to Stephansplatz

MARKETS

NASCHMARKT

Everything from truffles to oysters. On Saturday you can combine a visit to this food market (not to be confused with the Naschmarkt restaurant chain of the same name) with one to the flea market at the western end.

G7 ✉ Wienzeile, Kettenbrückengasse 🕐 Mon–Fri 6AM–6:30PM; Sat 6AM–5PM 🚇 U4 to Kettenbrückengasse

No-frills food

Cynics say that the favorite dish of a Viennese is a big one. The new self-service restaurants, however, offer much more flexibility in terms of portion size and in range of food (although the cuisine remains Austrian). Vienna's many ancient wine vaults also offer local wines and modestly priced food in a convivial and romantic setting. (A 15th-century writer remarked that more of Vienna was below ground than above it.) Sandwich bars offer open-sandwiches, a specialty here, and markets always have stalls selling snacks and delicacies.

COFFEE HOUSES

Coffee in cafés

The Viennese go to coffee houses to be alone, for which they need people around them, it is said. You can linger for hours and be asked to pay only when the waiter is going off shift. It is also a place to meet friends and exchange some of the gossip that is the motor of Viennese life. Some establishments offer billiards or a card game of Italian origin called tarock. Hot food is usually offered at very modest prices, and the standard dishes—typically such things as sausages or apfelstrudel—are always available.

See Vienna's Best
(► 59) for
BRÄUNERHOF
CAFÉ MUSEUM
CAFÉ CENTRAL
HAWELKA
LANDTMANN

CAFÉ MINISTERIUM ($)

Slightly down-at-heel café that's cozy for hot and filling lunches in winter.

✚ H6 ✉ Georg-Coch-Platz 4 ☎ 512 9225 🕐 Mon–Fri 7AM–11PM (breakfast until 11AM) 🚇 U1, U4 to Schwedenplatz 🚊 Trams 1, 2 on Ringstrasse

DIGLAS ($$)

Diglas was re-established as a café in the 1990s by the grandson of the original owner. Founded in 1923, it was a comparative latecomer to the coffee-house scene. Its most famous regular customer was the composer Franz Lehár.

✚ H6 ✉ Wollzeile 10 ☎ 512 8401 🕐 Daily 7AM–11PM 🚇 U1, U3 to Stephansdom

DOMMAYER ($$)

Vienna's oldest music café is the venue for matinée performances by the female ensemble Wiener Walzermädchen and other groups, as well as drama troupes. Close to Schönbrunn.

✚ B8 ✉ Auhofstrasse 2 (Hietzing) ☎ 877 5465 🕐 Daily 7AM–midnight 🚇 U4 to Hietzing

EILES ($)

Situated in a mainly residential area, this is a congenial, old-fashioned establishment with window seats and niches. Small menu at midday.

✚ G6 ✉ Josefstädter Strasse 2 ☎ 405 3410 🕐 Mon–Fri 7AM–10PM; Sat–Sun, hols 8AM–10PM 🚊 Tram J to Josefstädter Strasse

PRÜCKEL ($$)

The long tradition of cabaret performances continues in the basement, but Prückel also has piano music on Monday, Wednesday, and Friday evenings.

✚ H6 ✉ Stubenring 24 ☎ 512 43 39 🕐 9AM–10PM 🚇 U3 to Stubentor

SCHWARZENBERG ($$)

This is the oldest of the elegant Ringstrassen cafés, opened in 1861 when the boulevard was still under construction. There is a choice of newspapers, including foreign ones, and there are sybaritic touches, like the large selection of cigars for sale.

✚ H7 ✉ Kärntner Ring 17 ☎ 512 8998-13 🕐 Sun–Fri 7AM–midnight; Sat 9AM–midnight 🚊 Trams 1, 2 to Schwarzenbergplatz

TIROLERHOF ($)

Coffee houses were originally for men only, but this one had an exclusively female clientele as early as 1910. Now mixed, it is still a favorite among women.

✚ H6 ✉ Tegetthoffstrasse 8 (Albertinaplatz) ☎ 512 7833 🕐 Mon–Sat 7AM–9PM; Sun, hols 9:30AM–8PM 🚇 U1, U2, U4 to Oper

KONDITOREI

AIDA ($)
It's cramped, but the coffee and cakes are fine.

H6 ✉ Stock-im-Eisen-Platz 2 ☎ 512 2977 🕒 Mon–Sat 7AM–8PM; Sun 9AM–8PM 🚇 U1, U3 to Stephansplatz
Also at:
Bognergasse 3, Rotenturmstrasse 24, Wollzeile 28, and others

DEMEL ($$–$$$)
Founded in 1776 next to the now-demolished Burgtheater on Michaelerplatz, Demel nearly folded twice, the second time because of the revolution in 1848. Christoph Demel took over in 1857, and it remained in the family until Anna Demel's death in 1956. The staff were traditionally recruited from a convent in Währing and decked out in black uniforms with white frills. The lavish interior is a restoration dating from the 1930s (➤ 59).

G6 ✉ Kohlmarkt 14 ☎ 535 1717-39 🕒 Daily 10–7 🚇 U3 to Herrengasse

GERSTNER ($$–$$$)
A distinguished *Konditorei* that lures shoppers from Kärntner Strasse. Light lunches (expensive).

H6 ✉ Kärtner Strasse 11–15 ☎ 512 4963-77 🕒 Restaurant: Mon–Sat 10–8. Café: Mon–Sat 8:30–7 🚇 U1, U3 to Stephansplatz

HEINER ($$)
The branch overlooking Kärntner Strasse is excellent, but the little Biedermeier interior of Heiner in the Wollzeile is irresistible. The cakes and pastries are really superb, the coffee good. Special goodies for diabetics are available.

H6 ✉ Kärntner Strasse 21–3 ☎ 512 6863 🕒 Mon–Sat 8:30–7:30; Sun 10–7:30 🚇 U1, U3 to Stephansplatz
Also at:
H6 ✉ Wollzeile 9 ☎ 512 2343 🕒 Mon–Sat 8:30–7; Sun 10–7 🚇 U1, U3 to Stephansplatz

KONDITOREI LEHMANN ($$)
Elegant, but so popular that it's hard to get a seat. Good sandwiches as well as a large selection of pastries made on the premises.

H6 ✉ Graben 12 ☎ 512 1815 🕒 Mon–Sat 8:30–7 🚇 U1, U3 to Stephansplatz

KONDITOREI OBERLAAER STADTHAUS ($$)
Cognoscente assert that this relative newcomer to the city center is the best *Konditorei* of all. The premises are more spacious than many, and a light lunch is also available.

H6 ✉ Neuer Markt 16 ☎ 513 2936 🕒 Daily 8–11 🚇 U1, U3 to Stephansplatz

SLUKA ($$)
Another candidate for the title of Vienna's best, with mouth-watering pastries and light lunches.

G6 ✉ Rathausplatz 8 ☎ 405 7172 🕒 Mon–Fri 8–7; Sat 8–5:30 🚋 Tram J to Stadiongasse

Pastry shops

The *Konditorei* is another Viennese specialty, and pastry-makers have always been highly esteemed for their skills. The most distinguished in the city, Demel, was rewarded with the title *KK Hof-Zuckerbäckerei* (Imperial and Royal Confectioners). Zuckerbäcker were so much a part of the Viennese psyche that elaborate, over-ornamented architecture was referred to by locals as *Zuckerbäckerstil*, what would be called "wedding-cake style" in English.

INTERNATIONAL FARE

Alternatives

Apart from the Nordsee chain (➤ 65), there are a growing number of possibilities for serious fish eaters. For the freshest and best, you have to be prepared to dig deep in the pocket. The pizza trade expands even faster than hamburger joints in this part of the world, and there is now a good choice of places in central Vienna serving oven-fresh pizzas. There are even, in a city of mainly meat-eaters, some vegetarian restaurants.

ASIAN

AKAKIKO ($$)

Better value than many Japanese restaurants. The bonus here is the delightful roof terrace.
🕂 F7 ✉ Mariahilfer Strasse 40–48 (5th floor of Gerngross store) ☎ 524 0616 🕔 Mon–Sat 10:30–midnight; Sun 11–midnight 🚇 U3 to Neubaugasse

IMPERIAL GARDENS ($$$)

Hong Kong-style cuisine with seafood and duck specialties. The "as much as you can eat" buffet lunch is good value .
🕂 J6 ✉ Stubenring 18/Falkestrasse ☎ 512 4911 🕔 Mon–Sat 11:30–2:30, 6–11 🚇 U1, U2 to Stubentor

LUCKY PAVILLON ($$)

There are many Chinese restaurants in Vienna, one more dispiriting than another. This is an exception, and the dim sum is good.
🕂 J6 ✉ Löwengasse 21 ☎ 712 6293 🕔 11:30–3, 5:30–11:30 🚋 Tram N

SAFRAN ($$$)

If the need for a curry overwhelms you, this dignified restaurant with a wide range of Indian specialties will suit.
🕂 G5 ✉ Garnisongasse 10 ☎ 407 4234 🕔 Daily 11–3, 6–11.30 🚋 Trams 40, 41, 42 from Schottenton to Schwarzspanierstrasse

SIDDHARTHA ($$)

Regulars say this smart vegetarian restaurant, serving Indian based food, with red leather chairs and candles and flowers on the tables has the best chanterelles in town.
🕂 H6 ✉ Fleischmarkt 16 ☎ 513 1197 🕔 Tue–Sat 10:30–3, 6–11; Mon 11:30–3 🚇 U1, U4 to Schwedenplatz

TOKO-RI ($$)

This minute bar in Leopoldstadt has made a name for itself among sushi connoisseurs.
🕂 H5 ✉ Franz-Hochedlinger-Gasse 2 ☎ 214 8940 🕔 Mon–Sat noon–3, 6–11; Sun 6–11 🚇 U1, U4 to Schwedenplatz, then cross Salztorbrücke

EAST EUROPEAN

BODULO ($$)

A Croatian restaurant that serves fresh fish, simply prepared. Well worth the 2-mile trek out to Hernals.
🕂 C4 ✉ Hernalser Hauptstrasse 204 ☎ 486 4311 🕔 Tue–Sat 11–3, 5:30–11; Sun 11–3, 5:30–10 🚋 Tram 44 from Schottentor to last stop

ILONA–STÜBERL ($$)

Amazingly good value for stuffed cabbage, goulash, and other Hungarian fare. A plus is the *absence* of a Gypsy violinist playing with one elbow embedded in your goulash.
🕂 H6 ✉ Bräunerstrasse 2 ☎ 533 9029 🕔 Mon–Sat noon–3, 6–11 🚇 U1, U3 to Stephansplatz

KORNAT ($$–$$$)

This Croatian restaurant serves fish flown in fresh from the Dalmatian coast with wines from

Hvar and Korcula.

🔢 H6 ✉ Marc-Aurel-Strasse 8
☎ 535 6518 🕐 Mon–Sat
11:30–3, 6–midnight 🚇 U1,
U4 to Schwedenplatz

MEDITERRANEAN

ACHILLEUS ($$)

All the old Greek
favorites, from *mezedes* to
calamaris and *paidakia*
(lamb cutlets).

🔢 H6 ✉ Köllnerhofgasse 3
☎ 512 8328 🕐 Mon–Fri
5:30PM–noon; Sat–Sun
11:30AM–3PM, 5:30PM–11:30PM
🚇 U1, U3 to Stephansplatz

BODEGA ESPAÑOL ($)

A taste of Spain in the
heart of Vienna's 4th
district. *Tapas* like
pinchos de pollo con arroz
(skewers of grilled
chicken on rice) to wash
down with a good choice
of Spanish wines.

🔢 H8 ✉ Belvedergasse 10
☎ 504 5500 🕐 Tue–Fri
6PM–1AM 🚊 Tram D

KERVANSARAY ($$$)

Vienna's most renowned
fish restaurant with the
famous *Hummerbar*
(lobster bar). Upstairs is
a Turkish restaurant
where you can have a
more modest meal.

🔢 H7 ✉ Mahlerstrasse 9
☎ 512 8843 🕐 Mon–Sat noon
–midnight 🚇 U1, U2, U4 to Oper

ITALIAN

CANTINETTA
ANTINORI ($$$)

One of Vienna's oldest
Italian restaurants
owned by the Antinori
family, who produce
their own wines and
olive oil.

🔢 H6 ✉ Jasomirgottstrasse

3–5 ☎ 533 7722 🕐 Daily
11:30–2, 6–midnight 🚇 U1,
U3 to Stephansplatz

CASA ROMANA ($$)

This large pizzeria,
designed to evoke mem-
ories of the real thing,
serves authentic fare to
crowds of Italians.

🔢 H6 ✉ Rotenturmstrasse 17
☎ 535 2066 🕐 Daily
11AM–midnight 🚇 U1, U3 to
Stephansplatz

DA BIZI ($–$$)

A self-service system
allows you to assemble
the menu of your choice
(pasta, meat, salad, etc.).

🔢 H6 ✉ Rotenturmstrasse 4
☎ 513 3705 🕐 Daily
11AM–midnight 🚇 U1, U3 to
Stephansplatz

LA NINFEA ($$$)

Said to be the best
Italian restaurant in
Vienna, with a famed
wine list, and no, repeat
no, pizzas.

🔢 G6 ✉ Schauflergasse 6
☎ 532 9126 🕐 Mon–Sat
noon–3, 6–midnight. Closed Sun
🚇 U3 to Herrengasse

LA PIAZZA ($$)

Traditional pizza from a
wood-fired oven, plus
some Austrian dishes.

🔢 H6 ✉ Führichgasse 1
☎ 512 6255 🕐 Daily
2:30PM– midnight 🚇 U1, U2,
U4 to Oper

NOVELLI ($$$)

When you're tired of
pizza and pasta, look to
this lovely restaurant
with superb Italian fare
and wines to match.

🔢 H6 ✉ Bräunerstrasse 11
☎ 513 4200-1 🕐 Daily
noon–2, 6–11 🚇 U1, U3 to
Stephausplatz

Food from
around the world

Although Vienna has had a large
international community since
the 1970s, the choice of non-
Viennese cooking is not as great
as you might expect in a capital
city. True, the pizza and pasta is
ubiquitous, and the number of
Chinese and Japanese
restaurants is growing; yet there
are surprisingly few French
restaurants of repute, the Greek
and Spanish selection is
disappointing, and the cuisines of
some other territories are
virtually unknown. The list here
reflects the relative choice
available.

TEN BEST STORES

Bargains hard to find

When Austria entered the European Union in 1995, it was expected that prices would fall as a result of more penetration into a previously cartel-ridden and monopolists market. In some areas (chiefly where food is concerned) this has happened, but in luxury goods, prices are oriented to Munich or London, and there are no bargains. A tip is to try and buy non-exclusive goods outside the Innere Stadt, where prices are higher because the rents are high and many customers are well-to-do.

ALTMANN & KÜHNE
The maker of Vienna's best chocolates and the most creative candy.
H6 ✉ Graben 30 ☎ 533 0927 🕐 Mon–Fri 9–6:30; Sat 9–5 🚇 U1, U3 to Stephansplatz

ASENBAUM
Beautiful smaller antiques; the cultivated and knowledgable staff enhance the experience.
H6 ✉ Kärntner Strasse 28 ☎ 512 2847 🕐 Mon–Fri 10–6; Sat 10–1 🚇 U1, U3 to Stephansplatz

CHEGINI
A distinguished women's fashion store noted for its impeccable taste and selection.
H6 ✉ Kohlmarkt 7 ☎ 533 2058 🕐 Mon–Fri 9:45–6; Sat 10–1 🚇 U1, U3 to Stephansplatz

E. BRAUN & CO.
The bed and table linens were once sold to the Habsburg court. Also sells men's and women's clothing.
H6 ✉ Graben 8 ☎ 512 5505 🕐 Mon–Fri 9:15–6; Sat 9:15–1 🚇 U1, U3 to Stephansplatz

FREYTAG-BERNDT UND ARTARIA
Travel bookstore stocking English titles, especially books on Central Europe. Unrivaled selection of maps and street plans.
H6 ✉ Kohlmarkt 9 ☎ 533 8685 🕐 Mon–Fri 9–6:30; Sat 9–5 🚇 U3 to Herrengasse

GEBRÜDER WILD
Excellent lobsters, pâtés, caviar, and French wines—an epicurean's delight.
H6 ✉ Neuer Markt 10–11 ☎ 512 5303 🕐 Mon–Fri 8:30–6:30; Sat 8–12:30 🚇 U1, U3 to Stephansplatz

KNIZE
Exclusive men's tailors also notable for the 1913 facade and the interior designed by Adolf Loos.
H6 ✉ Graben 13 ☎ 512 2119 🕐 Mon–Fri 9:30–6; Thu 9:30–8; Sat 9:30–5 🚇 U1, U3 to Stephansplatz

SCHNEIDER & WARMUTH (HAIRDRESSERS)
The appropriately named Schneider (cutter) and Warmuth worked in the movie industry before becoming one of Vienna's most fashionable hair stylists.
F7 ✉ Kirchengasse 27 ☎ 522 6142 🕐 Tue–Wed 9–6; Thu–Fri 9–8; Sat 9–2 🚋 Tram 49 to Stiftgasse

STEFFL
Futuristic store interior arising from the ashes of the old Steffl, and now full of top labels. Media café, bar, and restaurant.
H6 ✉ Kärntner Strasse 19 ☎ 523 1756 🕐 Mon–Fri 9:30–7; Sat 9:30–5 🚇 U1, U3 to Stephansplatz

UNGER UND KLEIN
The best selection of wines from Lower Austria, Styria, and Burgenland.
H5 ✉ Gölsdorfgasse 2 ☎ 532 1323 🕐 Mon–Fri 9–6; Sat 11–2PM 🚇 U1, U4 to Schwedenplatz

ANTIQUES & ART GALLERIES

C. BEDNARCZYK
Specialist in 18th-century pieces. Paintings, glass, porcelain, and silver.
🔢 H6 ✉ Dorotheergasse 12 ☎ 512 4445 🕐 Mon–Fri noon–6; Sat 10–1 🚇 U1, U2, U4 to Oper

DOROTHEUM
An auction house founded in the 18th century in an old convent. You can find everything from the worthless to the priceless, some items marked for direct sale.
🔢 H6 ✉ Dorotheergasse 17 ☎ 515 600 🕐 Art auctions: Thu 2:30. Exhibitions of objects: Mon–Fri 10–6 🚇 U1, U2, U4 to Oper

ERNST HILGER
Contemporary Austrian art. Eleven special exhibitions each year.
🔢 H6 ✉ Dorotheergasse 5 ☎ 512 5315 🕐 Mon–Fri 12–6; Sat 10–1 🚇 U1, U3 to Stephansplatz

GALERIE HEIKE CURTZE
This gallery sells work by some of Austria's leading modern artists.
🔢 H6 ✉ Seilerstätte 15 ☎ 512 9375 🕐 Tue–Fri 3–7; Sat 11–2 🚇 U1, U3 to Stephansplatz

GALERIE HOFSTÄTTER
Contemporary Austrian art, and art nouveau.
🔢 H6 ✉ Bräunerstrasse 7 ☎ 512 3255 🕐 Mon–Fri 10–6; Sat 10–12:30 🚇 U1, U3 to Stephansplatz

GALERIE NÄCHST ST. STEPHAN
Avant-garde art from Austria and abroad.
🔢 H6 ✉ Grünangergasse 1 (runs between Singerstrasse and Schulerstrasse) ☎ 512 1266 🕐 Tue–Fri 10–6; Sat 11–2 🚇 U1, U3 to Stephansplatz

GALERIE NEBEHAY
Author, scholar, and collector Christian Nebehay is a leading expert on Klimt and Schiele. His store also sells old prints and antiquarian books, as well as his own (very useful) books on his specialist field—early 20th-century art.
🔢 H6 ✉ Annagasse 18 ☎ 512 1801 🕐 Mon–Fri 10–6; Sat 10–noon 🚇 U1, U2, U4 to Oper

GRITA INSAM
International avant-garde painting.
🔢 H6 ✉ Köllnerhofgasse 6 ☎ 512 5330 🕐 Tue–Fri 2–6; Sat 11–2 🚇 U1, U3 to Stephansplatz

RAUMINHALT
An unusual shop devoted to decorative objects and furniture of the last five decades. The 1950s are a specialty.
🔢 F6 ✉ Lange Gasse 19 ☎ 4090 9892 🕐 Mon–Fri 10–7; Sat 10–3 🚋 Tram J to Lederergasse

WIENER INTERIEUR
Compact store specializing in fine examples of smaller Jugendstil (▶ 58) and art-deco objects.
🔢 H6 ✉ Dorotheergasse 14 ☎ 512 2898 🕐 Mon–Fri 10–6; Sat 10–1 🚇 U1, U4, U2 to Oper

Famous art gallery
Galerie Nächst St. Stephan (✉ Grünangergasse 1 ☎ 512 1266) was started in 1954 by the the distinguished preacher Otto Mauer, who was devoted to reconciling the modern artist and the conservative Church. His gallery was the focus for discussion for liberal Catholics, including some who went on to lead the conservative Volkspartei (People's Party), in government in 2001. Church hierarchs admired Mauer's capacity for opening up a dialogue with the modern artist and the young, but feared any diminution of the Church's power.

CHINA, GLASS & HOME FURNISHINGS

Fine china

Since the 18th century or earlier, Vienna has produced a large quantity of objets d'art. The Secession (➤ 34), founded in 1897, was followed by the Wiener Werkstätte—its applied-art branch—and this gave renewed impetus to the creation of beautiful and functional items. The porcelain industry stretches back to the Habsburgs' encouragement of craft industries in the 18th century. The glassware from Lobmeyr, on the other hand, is the product of the 19th-century Historicism Movement, which fostered imitations of Renaissance and baroque models.

AUGARTEN

Porcelain with floral designs produced in Vienna at the factory in the park of the same name (➤ 56).

⊞ H6 ⊠ Stock-im-Eisen-Platz 3–4 ☎ 512 1494 ⏰ Mon–Fri 9–6; Sat 9–12:30 🚇 U1, U3 to Stephansplatz

WIENER PORZELLANFABRIK

You can also buy Augarten porcelain direct from the factory. Seconds sell at a 20 percent discount.

⊞ H4 ⊠ Wiener Porzellanmanufaktur, Obere Augartenstrasse 1 ☎ 211 240-18 ⏰ Mon–Fri 9–6; Sat 9–noon 🚋 Tram N

BACKHAUSEN

The inheritor of the Secession tradition has an extensive range of Wiener Werkstätte, along with Liberty patterns (patterns of the English Arts and Crafts Movement sold by Liberty of London).

⊞ H6 ⊠ Kärntner Strasse 33 ☎ 514 040 ⏰ Mon–Fri 9–6; Sat 9–5 🚇 U1, U3 to Stephansplatz

KERAMIK AUS GMÜNDEN

Gmünden in the Salzkammergut produces interesting ceramics with a touch of rusticity—green wavy lines on a white background—that is not to everyone's taste but is certainly exotic.

⊞ H6 ⊠ Kärntner Strasse 10 (Kärntner Durchgang) ☎ 512 5824 ⏰ Mon–Fri 9–6; Sat 9:30–5 🚇 U1, U3 to Stephansplatz

J. & L. LOBMEYR

The famous glassware is still made to the 19th-century neo-baroque and neo-Renaissance design. Above the store is a small exhibition of J. & L. Lobmeyr's early work.

⊞ H6 ⊠ Kärntner Strasse 26 ☎ 512 0508 ⏰ Mon–Fri 9–6; Sat 9–5 🚇 U1, U3 to Stephansplatz

RASPER & SÖHNE

A highly respected emporium for glass, porcelain, and cutlery, although some of the styles are an acquired taste.

⊞ H6 ⊠ Graben 15 ☎ 534 33-0 ⏰ Mon–Fri 9:30–6; Thu 9:30–8; Sat 9:30–5 🚇 U1, U3 to Stephansplatz

ROSENTHAL

The name needs no introduction for lovers of German-made china and glass.

⊞ H6 ⊠ Kärntner Strasse 16 ☎ 512 3994 ⏰ Mon–Fri 9:15–6; Sat 9:15–5 🚇 U1, U3 to Stephansplatz

WOKA

If you're looking for something with the flavor of the Wiener Werkstätte to take home, a reproduction lamp from this high quality workshop may be the answer.

⊞ H6 ⊠ Singerstrasse 16 ☎ 513 2912 ⏰ Mon–Fri 10–6; Sat 10–5 🚇 U1, U3 to Stephansplatz

CLOTHING

ADONIS

Young, fashionable leisurewear for men.

⊞ H6 ✉ Kohlmarkt 11 ☎ 533 7035 ◷ Mon–Fri 9–6; Sat 9:30–5 Ⓜ U1, U3 to Stephansplatz

ALEXANDER

Expensive, stylish, international sportswear and other clothing for both sexes.

⊞ H6 ✉ Rauhensteingasse 10 (between Himmelpfortgasse and Weihburggasse) ☎ 512 3946 ◷ Mon–Fri 9:30–6; Thu 9:30–8; Sat 9:15–5 Ⓜ U1, U3 to Stephansplatz

CASETTA-PAJOR

Good women's suits, plus a large selection of accessories.

⊞ J6 ✉ Landstrasser Hauptstrasse 1B ☎ 713 5118 ◷ Mon–Fri 9–6; Sat 9–5 Ⓜ U3 to Wien Mitte/Landstrasse Hauptstrasse

CHANEL BOUTIQUE (W. & A. JONAK)

The famous name.

⊞ H6 ✉ Trattnerhof 1 (off Graben) ☎ 533 9908 ◷ Mon–Fri 9:30–6; Thu 9:30–8; Sat 10–5 Ⓜ U1, U3 to Stephansplatz

ETOILE

Select stock of classic and idiosyncratic designs, including Armani and Kenzo.

⊞ H6 ✉ Lugeck 3 ☎ 512 6270 ◷ Mon–Fri 9:30–6; Sat 9:30–5 Ⓜ U1, U4 to Schwedenplatz

LODEN-PLANKL

The famous loden coats, which are well set off by a Tyrolean hat, are made with a technique using pressed felt. They are very stylish and warm and not so folkish that you cannot wear them outside Austria. But they do not come cheap.

⊞ G6 ✉ Michaelerplatz 6 ☎ 533 8032 ◷ Mon–Fri 9:30–6; Sat 9:30–4 Ⓜ U3 to Herrengasse, 2A to Michaelerplatz

MODUS VIVENDI

Wide selection of quality knitwear for the whole family, both made-to-measure and off the peg.

⊞ F7 ✉ Schadekgasse 4 ☎ 587 2823 ◷ Mon–Sat 9:30–5:30 Ⓜ U3 to Neubaugasse

RESI HAMMERER

Here you'll find *Trachtenmode* as well as haute couture. The owner skied on the Austrian national team.

⊞ H6 ✉ Kärntner Strasse 29–31 ☎ 512 6952 ◷ Mon–Fri 9:30–6; Thu 9:30–8; Sat 9:30–5 Ⓜ U1, U3 to Stephansplatz

TRACHTEN TOSTMANN

The place to go for a gift with a *Tracht* look. Departments for men, women, and children.

⊞ G5 ✉ Schottengasse 3 (Melkerhof) ☎ 533 5331 ◷ Mon–Fri 9–6:30; Sat 9–5 Ⓜ U2 to Schottentor

TRIXI BECKER

Elegant daywear and evening fashions with classical flair.

⊞ H6 ✉ Weihburggasse 4 ☎ 512 1749 ◷ Mon–Fri 9:30–6; Sat 9:30–5 Ⓜ U1, U3 to Stephansplatz

Trachtenmode

The basis of traditional Austrian dress is peasant and hunting costume. Women wear dirndls—dresses with full skirts and lace blouses that have a tight, revealing bodice—perhaps topped by a stylishly cut velvet jacket. Men wear green cloth jackets with braided cuffs and lapels, sometimes with buttons made from antlers. With its rural origins, and its rather showy Austrianness, *Trachtenmode* has definite right-wing associations. Still, it remains the uniform of the bourgeoisie and to some extent the nobility as well.

SHOES, LEATHER & LINGERIE

Costly leather

Fashion items such as leather goods are expensive in Vienna. The best selections and prices are found at chain stores like Humanic, in the vast shopping mall on the southern outskirts of the city (✉ Shopping City Süd, Vösendorf 🚍 Ikea bus from the Oper).

ANTONELLA
A large selection of shoes crammed into a small space.
✚ H6 ✉ Führichgasse 4
☎ 512 4173 🕐 Mon–Fri 9:30–6; Sat 9:30–5 🚇 U1, U3 to Stephansplatz

BALLY
One of several branches in Vienna of the first-rate shoe store.
✚ H6 ✉ Kärntner Strasse 9
☎ 512 1461 🕐 Mon–Fri 9–6; Thu 9–8; Sat 9–5 🚇 U1, U3 to Stephansplatz

BELLEZZA
Good shoes imported from Italy.
✚ H6 ✉ Kärntner Strasse 45
☎ 512 19 53 🕐 Mon–Fri 9:30–6; Sat 9:30–5 🚇 U1, U3 to Stephansplatz

DERBY-HANDSCHUHE
Devoted entirely to gloves. The fact that this store remains in business may have something to do with Viennese winters.
✚ H6 ✉ Plankengasse 5
☎ 512 5703 🕐 Tue–Fri 10–6; Sat 10–noon 🚇 U1, U3 to Stephansplatz

GEA
Shoes in a laid-back style. A local specialty is the Waldvierther ankle boot.
✚ H6 ✉ Himmelpfortgasse 26 ☎ 512 1969 🕐 Mon–Fri 10–6; Sat 10–5 🚇 U1, U3 to Stephansplatz

HUMANIC
Famous throughout the country for its surreal TV advertisements, this large chain offers a wide range of shoes at slightly less daunting prices than those of smaller stores.
✚ H6 ✉ Kärntner Strasse 51
☎ 512 5892 🕐 Mon–Fri 9:30–6; Sat 9:30–5 🚇 U1, U3 to Stephansplatz

PALMERS
Austria's most exotic lingerie comes from this chain, which is famous for its high-profile billboard advertising.
✚ H6 ✉ Kuhlmarkt 8–10
☎ 533 9204 🕐 Mon–Fri 9–6:30; Sat 9–5 🚇 U3 to Herrengasse

R. HORN
A cult store offering fine leather briefcases, handbags, wallets, and lots more for the chic man or woman about town .
✚ H6 ✉ Bräunerstrasse 7
☎ 513 8294 🕐 Mon–Fri 10–1, 2–6; Sat 10–5 🚇 U1, U3 to Stephansplatz

WALFORD
Over 50 years old, this company's tights and stockings have a worldwide reputation.
✚ H6 ✉ 1 Gonzagagasse 11
☎ 535 9900 🕐 Mon–Fri 9–6; Sat 10–5 🚇 U2, U4 to Shottenring

WEIN & WÄSCHE
This store is all about spoiling yourself, either with fine Italian and Austrian wines. or with that lacy little number you felt bold enough to buy after the second glass.
✚ H6 ✉ Lobkowitzplatz 3
☎ 512 9034 🕐 Mon–Fri 9:30–6; Sat 9:30–1 🚇 U1, U2, U4 to Karlsplatz

BOOKS & MUSIC

ARCADIA OPERA SHOP
The store for serious opera buffs, staffed by enthusiasts. Next to the opera.
✚ H7 ✉ Kärntner Strasse 40 ☎ 513 9568 🕐 Mon–Fri 9:30–6; Sat 9:30–5 🚇 U1, U2, U4 to Oper

BRITISH BOOKSHOP
An institution in Vienna. Large selection of books in English, plenty of Austriana, and stacks of novels and history books.
✚ H6 ✉ Weihburggasse 24–6 ☎ 512 1945 🕐 Mon–Fri 9–6; Sat 9–5 🚃 Trams 1, 2 to Weihburggasse

EMI AUSTRIA
Solid selection in all departments; especially strong on opera and classical music.
✚ H6 ✉ Kärntner Strasse 30 ☎ 512 3675-0 🕐 Mon–Fri 9:30–6; Sat 9:30–5 🚇 U1, U2, U4 🚃 Trams 1, 2 to Oper/Karlsplatz

FRICK
Primarily literature, with a large English department on the second floor. Paperbacks and children's books are strong points.
✚ H6 ✉ Graben 27 ☎ 533 9914 🕐 Mon–Fri 9–6; Sat 9–5 🚇 U1, U3 to Stephansplatz

GALERIE WOLFRUM
The specialist store for art books, with an excellent print department. Very knowledgable staff.
✚ H6 ✉ Augustinerstrasse 10 ☎ 512 5398 🕐 Mon–Fri 9:15–6; Sat 9:15–5 🚇 U1, U2, U4 to Oper

GEORG PRACHNER
The best store for books on architecture and the decorative arts, with material on Viennese art and architecture.
✚ H6 ✉ Kärntner Strasse 30 ☎ 512 8549-0 🕐 Mon–Fri 9:30–6; Sat 9:30–5 🚇 U1, U2, U4 to Oper

GEROLD
The large English department emphasizes politics and economics. You'll also find Austriana and books about Vienna.
✚ H6 ✉ Graben 31 ☎ 533 5014 🕐 Mon–Fri 9:15–6; Sat 9:15–5 🚇 U1, U3 to Stephansplatz

GRAMOLA
For opera lovers and those in search of historic performances on CD.
✚ H6 ✉ Graben 16 ☎ 533 5034 🕐 Mon–Fri 9:30–6; Sat 9:30–5 🚇 U1, U3 to Stephansplatz
Also at:
✚ H6 ✉ Kohlmarkt 5 ☎ 533 5047 🚇 U1, U3 to Stephansplatz

ROCK SHOP
A paradise for vinyl collectors. Oldies from the 1950s to the 1970s, mostly singles hits.
✚ J5 ✉ Taborstrasse 70 ☎ 216 8993 🕐 Mon–Fri 9–6; Sat 9–5 🚃 Tram N from Schwedenplatz to Heinestrasse

SHAKESPEARE & CO.
Plenty of trendy books from America. The local owners know their stuff.
✚ H6 ✉ Sterngasse 2 ☎ 535 5053 🕐 Mon–Wed, Fri 9–7; Thu 9–8; Sat 9–5 🚇 U1, U4 to Schwedenplatz

Book trade

Austria imposes Value Added Tax (*Mehrwertsteuer*) on books, which makes foreign paperbacks very expensive. Expect prices at least 50 percent above what you'd pay for a book in your own home town, and even more for newspapers. Austria's own publishing industry suffers from the small size of the local market, and from the dominance of big German firms, ever ready to scoop up promising Austrian authors for their lists.

THAT SPECIAL PRESENT

Viennese good taste

Part of the legacy of the Biedermeier and Jugendstil eras in Vienna is a talent for making simple things pleasing. This is reflected in the city's large choice of gifts, small artifacts, and clever design ideas, as well as in the skill with which they are packaged and presented. Sometimes, the style promises more than the substance delivers (this is what the Viennese call a *Schmäh*). At its best, however, Viennese design achieves a seductive combination of beauty and practicality.

HAAS & HAAS
Stylish gift shop that stocks candles, dried flowers, and delicate ornaments. Café.
✚ H6 ✉ Stephansplatz 4
☎ 513 1916 🕐 Mon–Fri 9–7:30; Sat 9–5 🚇 U1, U3 to Stephansplatz

HINTERMAYER
The king of remaindered books. The store is particularly welcome in Vienna since new books are formidably expensive.
✚ F7 ✉ Neubaugasse 27, 29, 36 ☎ 523 1057 🕐 Mon–Fri 9–6; Sat 9–5 🚇 U3 to Neubaugasse

KÖCHERT
Jewelers to the royal and imperial court since 1814. Elegant and restrained.
✚ H6 ✉ Neuer Markt 15
☎ 512 5828 🕐 Mon–Fri 9–6; Sat 9–5 🚇 U1, U3 to Stephansplatz

MARIA STRANSKY
Petit-point reticules, purses, and spectacle cases.
✚ G6 ✉ Hofburg, Burgpassage 2 ☎ 533 6098 🕐 Mon–Fri 9–6; Sat 9–5 🚇 U3 to Herrengasse 🚌 Hopper 2A to Michaelerplatz

MATERNS NATURBLUMENSALON
Artificial-flower posies, plus a good range of plants and cut flowers.
✚ G6 ✉ Herrengasse 10 ☎ 533 5460 🕐 Mon–Fri 8–6; Sat 8–5 🚇 U3 to Herrengasse

METZGER
Honey cake and candles.
✚ H6 ✉ Stephansplatz 7

☎ 512 3433 🕐 Mon–Fri 9–6; Sat 9–5 🚇 U1, U3 to Stephansplatz

NIEDERÖSTERREICH-ISCHES HEIMATWERK
Folk art from Lower Austria, including crafts, ceramics, and fabrics.
✚ G6 ✉ Herrengasse 6, Hochhaus ☎ 533 3495 🕐 Mon–Fri 9:30–6; Sat 9:30–5 🚇 U3 to Herrengasse

ÖSTERREICHISCHE WERKSTÄTTEN
Wide range of glass ornaments and gifts, with Secessionist (➤ 34) designs and attractive enamel. Be prepared for the aggressive sales people.
✚ H6 ✉ Kärntner Strasse 6 ☎ 512 2418 🕐 Mon–Fri 9:15–6; Sat 9:15–5 🚇 U1, U3 to Stephansplatz

SPITTELBERG MARKET
Local handicrafts are sold here on Saturdays from April to November, and daily just before Christmas.
✚ G7 ✉ Spittelberggasse 🕐 About 10AM–dusk 🚋 Tram 49 from Dr-Karl-Renner-Ring to Stiftgasse

TOSTMANN
Gifts inspired by folk art: hollow glass candlesticks, silvered inside (*Bauernsilber*—peasant silver), are a specialty. Next door to the *Tracht* clothes store (➤ 73).
✚ G5 ✉ Schottengasse 3A ☎ 533 5331 🕐 Mon–Fri 9–6:30; Sat 9–12:30 🚇 U2 to Schottentor 🚋 Trams 1, 2

FOOD & DRINK

ANKER

Fresh bread, excellent cakes and pastries. Central branches in Stock-im-Eisen-Platz, Bräuner Strasse, and Wollzeile. Branches at train termini have longer hours and Sunday opening. Many have a counter for a snack or even *Kaiserfrühstuck* (Emperor's breakfast). 🕐 Mon–Fri 7:30–6; Sat 8–5

DEMMERS TEEHAUS

The genuine Chinese or Indian teas available here will please those who are dispirited by the tea bag and hot water that is sold as "tea" in cafés. There is a tea salon upstairs. Several branches. ✚ G5 ✉ Mölker Bastei 5 ☎ 533 5995 🕐 Mon–Wed, Fri 9–6:30; Thu 9–8; Sat 9–5. Closed Sun 🚇 U2 to Schottentor 🚋 Trams 1, 2

DIE WEINBAUERN

Over 140 growers offer products for tasting at this store—brandies, Schnapps, and *Sekt*, as well as wine. Since the 1980s, when it was found that glycol had been added to wines to make them sweeter, Austrian wine has the strictest production regulations in Europe, and its quality is often overlooked. Good value. ✚ G7 ✉ Schleifmühlgasse 15 ☎ 586 9049 🕐 Mon–Fri 10–6:30; Sat 10–5 🚇 U1, U2, U4 to Karlsplatz

JULIUS MEINL AM GRABEN

A fine grocer with a superb delicatessen counter and a very expensive buffet (open two hours longer than the shop). ✚ H6 ✉ Graben 19 ☎ 532 3334 🕐 Mon–Fri 8:30–7; Sat 8–5 🚇 U1, U3 to Stephansplatz

NATURKOST ST. JOSEF

Organic food, including items such as South American quinoa. ✚ F7 ✉ Zollergasse 26 ☎ 526 6818 🕐 Mon–Fri 8–6:30; Thu 8–8; Sat 8–5 🚇 U3 to Neubaugasse

NATURPRODUKTE ENGELBERT PERLINGER

Whole and organic foods, alternative beauty therapies, and baby food. Several branches. ✚ G8 ✉ Wiedner Hauptstrasse 66 ☎ 586 0671 🕐 Mon–Fri 9–6; Sat 9–5 🚋 Trams 62, 65

SCHÖNBICHLER

This is where the Viennese buy their English marmalade, tea, Scotch whisky, and Christmas pudding. ✚ H6 ✉ Wollzeile 5 ☎ 512 1868 🕐 Mon–Fri 8:30–6; Sat 8:30–5 🚇 U1, U3 to Stephansplatz

VINOTHEK BEI DER PIARISTENKIRCHE

Only the best Austrian wines (which usually means Grüner Veltliner, Riesling or Weissburgunder—all whites) are sold in this exclusive store. ✚ F6 ✉ Piaristengasse 54 ☎ 405 9553 🕐 Mon–Fri 2:30–6; Sat 9–5 🚌 Bus 13A; tram J to Lederer Gasse

Where to buy your Sachertorte

The origin of Sachertorte is so hotly disputed that there have been lawsuits between rival claimants. Those who want authenticity buy at Sacher (✉ Philharmonikerstrasse 4 ☎ 514 56-0 🕐 Mon–Sat 9AM–11PM; Sun 3PM–6PM. They will also mail). The Hotel Imperial (► 84) also lays claim to the recipe but calls it the Imperial Torte. On the other hand, you can buy a perfectly acceptable Sachertorte for much less at any branch of Aida (► 67).

SPORTS

Sporting culture

The Viennese are not great sportsmen; those who are, flee to the mountains for skiing (Semmering and the Annaberg in Lower Austria are a couple of hours away). However, the Socialist-run Vienna of the 1920s "Rotes Wien" made conspicuous efforts to develop an *Arbeiterkultur* (workers' culture) in contradistinction to middle-class pursuits. This included physical culture, and many of the city's pools date from this period. An example of this is Amalienbad (✉ Reumannplatz 23 ☎ 607 4747 ⏰ Tue–Sun 7:30–8), an architecturally intriguing pool and building with marvelous art-deco designs.

WIENER STADTHALLE (HALLE C)

Major municipal sports complex with an ice rink and Olympic-sized swimming pool.
✚ E7 ✉ Vogelweidplatz 14 ☎ 981 000 ⏰ Mon–Fri 1:30–5; Sat–Sun, hols 8–noon, 1–5 🚇 U6 🚊 Tram 49 to Burggasse/ Stadthalle/Urban-Loritz-Platz

BOWLING

BRUNSWICK BOWLING
✚ D4 ✉ Schumanngasse 107 ☎ 486 4361 🚊 Tram 42 from Schottentor to Hildebrandgasse

BOWLINGHALLE PRATER
✚ K6 ✉ Prater Hauptallee 124 ☎ 728 0709 🚊 Tram N from Schwedenplatz to last stop

CYCLING

PEDAL POWER
Delivery, pick-up, and map with self-guided tour suggestions. Group tours of the city.
✚ J5 ✉ Ausstellungsstrasse 3 ☎ 729 7234 🚇 U1 to Praterstern 🚊 Tram O

GOLF

CITY & COUNTRY GOLF CLUB AM WEINERBERG
In the southern suburbs of Vienna.
✚ Off map at G10 ✉ Gutheil Schoder-Gasse 9 ☎ 661 23 🚌 Bus 16A to Gutheil Schoder-Gasse

THE VIENNA GOLF CLUB
More demanding socially than in terms of sporting skills.
✚ N8 ✉ Rennbahnstrasse 65A, Freudenau ☎ 728 9564-0; fax 728 5379 ⏰ 7:30AM– dusk 🚌 Bus 77A from Rennweg/Ungargasse

HORSE RACING

Racing attracts people from all classes. Flat races and steeplechases are held at Freudenau from spring to fall.
✚ N8 ✉ Rennbahnstrasse 65, Freudenau ☎ 728 9535; fax 728 95 17 🚌 Bus 77A from Rennweg/Ungargasse

ICE-SKATING

WIENER EISLAUFVEREIN
✚ H7 ✉ Lothringerstrasse 22 ☎ 713 6353 ⏰ Oct–Mar: Sat–Mon 9–8; Tue, Thu, Fri 9–9; Wed 9–10 🚇 U4 to Stadtpark

WATERSPORTS

STRANBAD ALTE DONAU
River swimming on the "old" arm of the Danube, now bypasssed.
✚ H7 ✉ Lothringerstrasse 22 ☎ 713 6353 ⏰ Sep–Mar: Mon–Tue, Thu–Sat 9AM–9PM; Wed 9AM–10PM; Sun, hols 9AM–8PM 🚊 Trams D, 71

FRITZ EPPEL
Boats to rent.
✚ L3 ✉ Wagramer Strasse 48 ☎ 263 3530 🚇 U1 to Alte Donau

KARL HOFBAUER
Rowboats and sailboats for rent. Also has a sailing school.
✚ M2 ✉ An der Oberen Alten Donau 184–186 ☎ 238 2853 🚇 U1 to Kagran

THEATER

AKADEMIETHEATER
Sister-theater to the Burgtheater, the superb Akademietheater has a generally, but not exclusively, modern repertoire of serious plays and a number of translated works.
✚ H7 ✉ Lisztgasse 1 ☎ 51 444 Ⓤ U4 to Stadtpark

BURGTHEATER
If you speak German, try to include a visit. Otherwise, join a tour to see the Gustav and Ernst Klimt frescoes (► 31).
✚ G6 ✉ Dr-Karl-Lueger-Ring 2 ☎ 51 444 Trams 1, 2 to Burgtheater, Rathaus

INTERNATIONAL THEATER
A small theater known for good entertainment. It sometimes has a surprise hit on its hands —for example, that most challenging of dramas, *The Mousetrap*, proved as popular in Vienna as in London.
✚ G5 ✉ Porzellangasse 8 ☎ 319 6272 Tram D to Schlickgasse

KAMMERSPIELE
This subsidiary stage of the Theater in der Josefstadt puts on plays, lighter fare—often comedies and farces, not infrequently recycled London hits.
✚ H6 ✉ Rotenturmstrasse 20 ☎ 427 00-300 Ⓤ U1, U4 to Schwedenplatz

SERAPIONS THEATERVEREIN
If you don't speak German, this is undoubtedly the place for a theatrical evening out. The amazingly accomplished mime rivals Marcel Marceau's for imaginative brilliance. The performances are poetic, symbolic, ironic, sad, and often intensely moving.
✚ H5 ✉ Odeon Theater, Taborstrasse 10 ☎ 214 5562-20 Tram N from Schwedenplatz to Karmeliterplatz

THEATER IN DER JOSEFSTADT
Once the powerhouse of the famous player-director, Max Reinhardt, who co-founded the Salzburg Festival, this theater designed by Joseph Kornhäusel in the 1820s is especially close to Viennese hearts. Outside, plaques honor Reinhardt and Hugo von Hofmannsthal, the latter a leading 20th-century dramatist and the librettist for several operas by Richard Strauss. Jugendstil (► 58) drama is still played here constantly.
✚ F6 ✉ Josefstädterstrasse 26 ☎ 427 00-300 Tram J

VIENNA'S ENGLISH THEATRE
Solid productions of mainstream drama from England and America, given a bit of pep by visiting stars. Thoroughly worthy and occasionally heights-scaling.
✚ F6 ✉ Josefsgasse 12 ☎ 402 1260 Ⓤ U2 to Lerchenfelderstrasse

Outrage and excellence

From 1986 until 1999, the Burgtheater—the flagship of Austrian drama—was under the direction of Claus Peymann, a German whose radical productions and prejudiced political statements were inimical to the Austrian establishment. Resignations ensued when he imported 80 German actors, and although his contract was renewed, his application for Austrian citizenship was turned down. He was known for his challenging and imaginative productions of contemporary drama and the classics, and for nurturing the talent of Thomas Bernhard, Austria's greatest contemporary writer. His successor, after a successful spell at the Volkstheater, has adopted a lower profile.

OPERA, OPERETTA & MUSICALS

The musical tradition

Music has been part of the city's culture from earliest times. In the mid-18th century Haydn and then Mozart began to displace the long-dominant Italians in public esteem. The 19th century was also rich in musical talent, some of it imported (Beethoven, Brahms) but much home-grown (Schubert, Brückner, Hugo Wolf, Strauss father and son, and Mahler). Later, Arnold Schönberg pioneered the 12-tone system, while his erstwhile-pupils, such as Alban Berg and Anton von Webern, made the "Second Viennese School" world famous.

ETABLISSEMENT RONACHER

This marvelous old variety theater, with an exotic late 19th-century interior, has reopened after a long period of darkness. Its program remains unpredictable— from a spectacular à la André Heller (➤ 9) to a Broadway musical.
🕂 H6 ✉ Himmelpfortgasse 25 ☎ 514 110 🚇 U1, U3 to Stephansplatz

RAIMUND THEATER

Named for the great comedian and dramatist, Ferdinand Raimund (1790–1836), the theater stages operettas and musicals. Built in 1893, it has an alarmingly precipitous stacking of gallery seats.
🕂 E8 ✉ Wallgasse 18–20 ☎ 599 770 🚇 U3 to Westbahnhof

SCHÖNBRUNNER SCHLOSSTHEATER

In the rococo theater where Haydn and Mozart once conducted, the Wiener Kammeroper performs lighter opera and operettas during July and August.
🕂 C8 ✉ Schloss Schönbrunn (main entrance) ☎ 877 3136 🚇 U4 to Schönbrunn

STAATSOPER

The State Opera reopened in 1955 with a performance of Beethoven's *Fidelio*; appropriately enough, the last performance before it closed in 1944 was Wagner's *Götterdämmerung* (*Twilight of the Gods*). It remains one of the world's top opera stages.
🕂 H7 ✉ Opernring 2 ☎ 51 444 🚇 U1, U2, U4 to Oper

THEATER AN DER WIEN

Original owner Emanuel Schikaneder, librettist for Mozart's *Magic Flute*, complained that he had written "such a good piece, but Mozart ruined it all with his music." A shrewd impresario, Schikaneder would have appreciated the theater's success with such musicals as *Cats*, which ran for 11 years.
🕂 G7 ✉ Linke Wienzeile 6 ☎ 588 300 🚇 U1, U2, U4 to Karlsplatz

VOLKSOPER

Even though it's in the uncongenial area of the Gürtel (Ring Road), the Volksoper is no poor relation of the Staatsoper. It may not have the budget to engage prima donnas, but its Mozart performances are solid and often inspired. The tickets cost less, too.
🕂 F4 ✉ Währinger Strasse 78 ☎ 51 444 🚇 U6 to Volksoper 🚊 Trams 40, 41 42

WIENER KAMMEROPER

A seedbed for talent for the Volksoper, Staatsoper or abroad. The program includes many lesser-known operas, sometimes abridged.
🕂 H6 ✉ Fleischmarkt 24 ☎ 513 6072 🚇 U1, U4 to Schwedenplatz

ORCHESTRAL MUSIC

ARNOLD SCHÖNBERG CENTER

Not only a concert hall, but also an archive library and exhibition hall dedicated to the founder of Vienna modernism.

✚ H7 ✉ Zaunergasse 1–3
☎ 712 1888-50 🚋 Trams 1, 2 to Schwarzenbergplatz

BÖSENDORFER SAAL

A venue for chamber-music concerts named after Vienna's most celebrated dynasty of piano-makers.

✚ H8 ✉ Graf-Starhemberg-Gasse 14 ☎ 504 6651 🚇 U1 to Taubstummengasse 🚋 Trams 62, 65

KONZERTHAUS

Opened in 1913, the building contains three concert halls: the Grosser Saal, for orchestral performances; and the Mozartsaal and the Schubertsaal for chamber music, modern music, and Lieder evenings. In summer there are twice-weekly selections of Mozart's music, played by musicians dressed in period costume.

✚ H7 ✉ Lothringerstrasse 20
☎ 712 1211 🚇 U4 to Stadtpark

MUSIKVEREIN

The Musikverein is famous for its superb acoustics and sumptuous gilded interior (caryatids to the right and left of you). The Wiener Philharmoniker's New Year's Day Concert is broadcast from here and the orchestra's Sunday concerts are a Viennese

institution. During the week there are orchestral concerts in the Great Hall, and chamber music in the Brahmssaal.

✚ H7 ✉ Bösendorferstrasse 12 ☎ 505 8190 🚇 U1, U2, U4 to Karlsplatz

ÖSTERREICHISCHE GESELLSCHAFT FÜR MUSIK

An intimate concert hall for an evening of chamber music or Lieder.

✚ G6 ✉ Hanuschgasse 3
☎ 512 3143 🚇 U1, U2, U4 to Karlsplatz

PALACES

The city's summer music festival, Wiener Musik-Sommer, offers graceful chamber music in some lovely baroque palaces, among them Palffy, Auersperg, and Schwarzenberg. The Strauss summer festival takes place inside the opulent original Stock Exchange in Palais Ferstel (▶ 38).

RADIO KULTURHAUS

The Radio Symphonie-orchester (and other ensembles) supplies varied classical music that is generally very good.

✚ H8 ✉ Argentinierstrasse 30A ☎ 5017 0377 🚇 Bus 13A

URANIA

A multicultural education and performance center with a concert hall for recitals.

✚ J6 ✉ Uraniastrasse 1
☎ 712 6191-0 🚇 U1, U4 to Schwedenplatz

Musical taste

The Musikverein—the concert hall for the Society of the Friends of Music—was founded in the 19th century. Mainstream Viennese taste is conservative ("The popularity of Brahms," wrote one critic, "is due largely to his music being exactly suited to Viennese tastes, not too hot and not too cold; it eschews excitement and seldom commits the unforgivable sin of being boring.") But there has always been a radical element. The greatest scandal in the Musikverein's history occurred in 1913 when pro- and anti-modernists began fighting at a Schönberg concert.

JAZZ & NIGHTSPOTS

Night music

You can now hear most types of jazz regularly in Vienna. In summer there is a jazz festival held partly in the hallowed Staatsoper (▶ 80), and there is an open-air festival on the Donau-Insel (Danube Island) in July. Performances generally start at 9PM but check the current *Wien Programm* (available at all Tourist Information Bureaux). The night scene has grown livelier and the Bermuda Dreieck (Bermuda Triangle, ▶ 18) is a magnet for gilded youth. You will find there idiosyncratic bars, trendy restaurants, discos, beer cellars, live music, and cabaret.

ARENA

A music and arts center that includes jazz in its avant-garde repertoire.

➕ L8 ✉ Baumgasse 80 ☎ 798 8595 🚇 U3 to Erdberg

CAFÉ VOLKSGARTEN

A favored venue, especially in summer, in an attractive setting, with an open-air dance floor.

➕ G6 ✉ Burgring 1 ☎ 533 0518 🕐 Sun–Thu 8PM–2AM; Fri–Sat 8PM–4AM 🚇 U3 🚋 Trams 1, 2 to Dr-Karl-Renner-Ring/Bellaria Strasse

JAZZLAND

Traditional jazz from some of the best bands in town in an ancient basement under the Ruprechtskirche (▶ 51).

➕ H5 ✉ Franz-Josefs-Kai 29 ☎ 533 2575 🚇 U1, U4

NIGHTFLY'S CLUB

A cozy basement bar where you'll hear golden oldies, from Glenn Miller to Frank Sinatra.

➕ H6 ✉ Dorotheergasse 14 ☎ 512 9979 🕐 Winter–Spring: Mon–Sat 8PM–3AM. Summer: Mon–Sat 6PM–3AM 🚇 U1, U3 to Stephansplatz

PAPAS TAPAS

A jazz room at a venue with a disco. Also country and rhythm and blues evenings.

➕ H7 ✉ Schwarzenbergplatz 10 ☎ 505 0311 🚋 Trams D, 1, 2 to Schwarzenbergplatz

ROTER ENGEL

"The Red Angel" exemplifies the best of the Bermuda Dreieck. It calls itself a *Wein und Liederbar* (wine and song bar) and serves drinkable wines with cheeses. It also has folk and rhythm and blues evenings.

➕ H6 ✉ Rabensteig 5 ☎ 535 4105 🕐 Mon–Sat 5PM–2 or 4AM 🚇 U1, U4 🚋 Trams 1, 2 to Schwedenplatz

SZENE WIEN

Visiting rock bands and dance companies perform at this co-operative established by politically engaged musicians. Wear your leather jackets.

➕ Off map at L10 ✉ Hauffgasse 26 ☎ 749 3341 🕐 Generally 8PM 🚋 Tram 71 to Kopalgasse from Schwarzenbergplatz

U4

An enduring and continually fashionable dance club with live music most nights. Next door is a luxurious bar.

➕ E9 ✉ Schönbrunner Strasse 222 ☎ 815 8307 🕐 11PM–5AM 🚇 U4 to Meidlinger Hauptstrasse

VORSTADT

Look for an interesting mixture of jazz, ethnic music, and cabaret.

➕ E6 ✉ Herbststrasse 37 ☎ 493 1788 🕐 Generally 8PM 🚌 Bus 48A from Dr-Karl-Renner-Ring to Kirchenstetterngasse

WUK

Arts center with café and restaurant, and also performance art, dance, and DJ nights.

➕ G5 ✉ Währinger Strasse 59 ☎ 401 2170 🕐 Opening times vary, phone for details 🚋 Trams 40, 41, 42 from Schottentor

CONNOISSEURS' VIENNA

ALTE SCHMIEDE
This old blacksmith's workshop is now a venue for readings, workshops, "artotheque," and some cool modern music.
H6 ⊠ Schönlaterngasse 9 ☎ 512 4446 ⏰ Generally 7PM U1, U3 to Stephansplatz

AMERICAN KÄRNTNER BAR (LOOS BAR)
This famously tiny bar is a late-night watering hole designed by Secessionist Adolf Loos.
H6 ⊠ Kärntner Durchgang (off Kärntner Strasse 10) ☎ 512 3283 ⏰ Sun–Thu 6PM–2AM; Fri–Sat 7PM–4AM U1, U3 to Stephansplatz

BEATRIXSTÜBERL
So it's been a hard day's night, The Beatrix is the answer, with solid Austrian food at breakfast time. On weekends, there's rock music in the Beatrix Keller.
J7 ⊠ Ungargasse 8 ☎ 712 5876 ⏰ Mon–Fri 10AM–8AM; 7:30PM–8AM Tram 71 from Schwarzenbergplatz

KRAH KRAH
Some 55 different brands of beer, and hefty black-bread sandwiches.
H6 ⊠ Rabensteig 8 ☎ 533 8193 ⏰ Daily 11AM–2AM U1, U4 to Schwedenplatz

LOBAU
Although topless bathing is unlikely to raise an eyebrow, nudity remains the province of enthusiasts for FKK (*Freikörperkultur*—naturism). The Lobau is a naturist area on the Neue Donau (Danube) southeast of the city.
Off map at N6 ⊠ Neue Donau U1 to Kaisermühlen, then Bus 91A to the Zum Roten Hiasl inn

ÖSTERREICHISCHES FILMMUSEUM
The dedicated Austrian Film Museum has kept this shrine to the movies alive. Pay the low membership fee, then a modest entrance charge.
H6 ⊠ Albertina-Augustinerstrasse 1 ☎ 533 7054-0 ⏰ Programs and times posted at the entrance U1, U2, U4 to Oper

RÖMER SAUNA
Sauna, bar, and café in the center of town.
H6 ⊠ Passauerplatz 6 ☎ 533 5318 U1, U4 to Schwedenplatz

SALZAMT
This designer restaurant continues to draw artists and cultural trendies. Even the food is good.
H6 ⊠ Ruprechtsplatz 1 ☎ 533 5332 ⏰ Daily 5PM–1AM U1, U4 to Schwedenplatz

SCHAU SCHAU
Custom-made glasses by a master of the art: rims of acetate, buffalo-horn, metal, and 18-karat gold moulded in styles that range from the classical to the decidedly outré. A shopping haunt of the "promis" and "glitterati" on the Viennese social scene.
H6 ⊠ Rotenturmstrasse 11 ☎ 533 5484 ⏰ Mon–Fri 8:30–6 U1, U4 to Schwedenplatz

Well-kept secrets
Geheimtips—things that the initiates prefer to keep to themselves—are by definition inclined to be ephemeral. This page describes what might be called perennial *Geheimtips*—places that have established themselves as having something special to offer. They give a flavor of the Vienna beyond the superficial glitter it so willingly displays for tourists.

The gay and lesbian scene
Look into the stylish Café Savoy (⊠ Linke Wienzeile 36 ☎ 586 7348) with an opulent interior or the Café Berg (⊠ Bergasse 8 ☎ 319 5720), a long established café adjacent to a bookshop (Lowenherz) with gay and feminist literature. More information on the gay and lesbian scene appear in the monthly publications *Extra*, *Bussi*, and *Vienna Gay Guide*, which are available at most gay venues around the city.

LUXURY HOTELS

Prices

Expect to pay the following prices per night for a double room with breakfast:

$$$	over AS3,500; 218 euros
$$	AS2,000–3,000; 109–218 euros
$	AS900–1,500; 65–109 euros

Sacher Hotel

Sacher was once famous for its *chambres séparées*, where aristocrats "entertained" dancers. It was founded in 1876 by the son of the cook to Prince Metternich and carried on by his formidable, cigar-smoking widow, Anna, who ruled her hotel and guests with an iron rod. Just after World War I, Anna single-handedly held off a mob of rioting workers, but she also had a strong social conscience and fed the poor from the kitchen.

BRISTOL ($$$)

Old-fashioned elegance on the Ringstrasse. Its restaurant, Korso bei der Oper (▶ 62), is one of the best in Vienna.
➕ H7 ✉ Kärntner Ring 1
☎ 515 16-0; fax 5151 650
🚇 U1, U2, U4 to Oper

IM PALAIS SCHWARZENBERG ($$$)

Located in the Fischer von Erlachs' palace (▶ 53), this is probably the most elegant address in Vienna. Lovely restaurant (▶ 62).
➕ H7 ✉ Schwarzenbergplatz 9
☎ 798 4515; fax 798 4714
🚋 Tram D to Prinz EugenStrasse

IMPERIAL ($$$)

This former palace on the Ringstrasse is also the *Staatshotel* (official State Hotel) where visiting dignitaries stay. Hitler lodged here just after the *Anschluss*.
➕ H7 ✉ Kärntner Ring 16
☎ 501 10-0; fax 5012 3410
🚇 U1, U2, U4 to Karlsplatz
🚋 Trams 1, 2 to Schwarzenbergplatz

INTER-CONTINENTAL WIEN ($$$)

You'll find a bit more than chain-hotel efficiency here. A bonus is the superb Vier Jahreszeiten restaurant (▶ 62).
➕ H7 ✉ Johannesgasse 28
☎ 711 22-0; fax 713 4489
🚇 U4 to Stadtpark

MARRIOTT VIENNA ($$$)

The postmodern architecture harmonizes reasonably well with its surroundings. The business facilities are unrivaled.
➕ H6 ✉ Parkring 12A
☎ 515 18-0; fax 515 18-6736
🚇 U3 to Stubentor

PLAZA–HILTON WIEN ($$$)

An attractive luxury hotel built in neo-Secessionist style with all modern comforts (▶ 58).
➕ G5 ✉ Schottenring 11
☎ 313 90-0 🚇 U2 🚋 Trams 1, 2 to Schottenring

RADISSON SAS-PALAIS HOTEL ($$$)

Distinguished hotel famous for solid service and its excellent restaurant, La Siècle im Ersten.
➕ H6 ✉ Palais Heckel von Donnersmarck, Weihburggasse 32, Parkring 16 ☎ 515 17-0; fax 512 2216 🚇 U3 to Stubentor

RENAISSANCE WEIN ($$$)

The latest to make it into the luxury class of Viennese hotels, this is slightly impersonal but has an indoor pool and many other facilities. Close to the traffic hub of Meidling Hauptstrasse.
➕ E9 ✉ Vllmanustrasse 71
☎ 891 02-0 🚇 U4 to Meidling Hauptstrasse

SACHER ($$$)

Room sizes may not be generous, but Sacher is Vienna's most celebrated hotel—and not only because of the cake.
➕ H6
✉ Philharmonikerstrasse 4
☎ 514 56-0; fax 514 57-810
🚇 U1, U2, U4 to Oper

HOTELS OF LOCAL CHARACTER

ALTSTADT VIENNA ($$)
Small but refined, the beautifully furnished upper floors of this 18th-century house are an informal, friendly breakfast-only hotel.
🔆 F7 ☒ Kirchengasse 41 ☎ 526 3399-0; fax 523 4901 🚌 Bus 48A from Dr-Karl-Renner-Ring

ALTWIENERHOF ($$)
This one is for food lovers; rates for a room with breakfast and one meal are a bargain, in view of the fine restaurant (► 62). The nine rooms have an opulent belle-époque look.
🔆 E8 ☒ Herklotzgasse 6 ☎ 892 6000 🚇 U3, U6 to Westbahnhof

DORINT BIEDERMEIER WEIN ($$)
This period townhouse, with Biedermeier furniture is an oasis of tranquillity in the Landstrasse area.
🔆 J7 ☒ Landstrasser Hauptstrasse 28, Ungargasse 13 ☎ 716 71-0 🚇 U3, U4 to Wien Mitte, Landstrasser Hauptstrasse

DAS TRIEST ($$$)
Terence Conran meets Wiener Modern. Conran's postmodern conversion of an old coaching inn has an excellent restaurant.
🔆 G7 ☒ Wiedner Hauptstrasse 12 ☎ 58 918 🚋 Trams 62, 65 to first stop on Wiedner Hauptstrasse

GARTENHOTEL GLANZING ($$)
A 1920s cube-like villa softened by climbing vines. Peaceful but far from the center.
🔆 D2 ☒ Glanzinggasse 23 ☎ 470 4272 🚌 Bus 35A to Krottenbachstrasse

HOTEL AM SCHUBERTRING ($$)
Has a welcoming Adolf Loos-style bar for musicians. No restaurant.
🔆 H7 ☒ Schubertring 11 ☎ 717 02-0; fax 713 9966 🚋 Trams 1, 2 to Schwarzenbergplatz

HOTEL RÖMISCHER KAISER ($$)
A modest baroque palace in the old city. Delightful—all crimson fabrics and chandeliers. No restaurant.
🔆 H6 ☒ Annagasse 16 ☎ 512 7751-0; fax 512 7751-13 🚇 U1, U3 to Stephansplatz

KAISERIN ELISABETH ($$)
With its location close to Stephansplatz this place with a whiff of imperial nostalgia is a firm favorite with regular Vienna visitors. A good choice if you want to be immersed in the Altstadt atmosphere.
🔆 H6 ☒ Weinburggasse 3 ☎ 515 26-0; fax 515 26-7 🚇 U1, U3 to Stephansplatz

KÖNIG VON UNGARN ($$$)
An 18th-century building next to the Figarohaus. Rooms ring an airy, glassed-in courtyard. Prestigious restaurant.
🔆 H6 ☒ Schulerstrasse 10 ☎ 515 84-0 🚇 U1, U3 to Stephansplatz

Charm and comfort

The formula of most luxury hotels does not differ much from country to country. More unusual is the individual environment that not only bears the stamp of the owner's persona but exploits the particular characteristics of the local culture. In Vienna such hostelries often occupy a baroque or Biedermeier building, so that the hotel combines all the charm of the original with all the comforts of modernity.

MID-RANGE & BUDGET ACCOMMODATIONS

In search of good value

Other than youth hostels, there are very few inexpensive accommodations in Vienna. At the same time, there are still hotels with less than friendly service that nevertheless charge the (high) going rate. The Viennese themselves remark darkly that the world of hotels is under the eternal sway of the mythical "King Nepp" (from *neppen*, meaning to overcharge). Few escape his tyrannous rule, but there are several (some of which are listed here) that do try hard to offer value for money and friendly service.

HOTEL JÄGER ($$)

A welcoming hotel in a large villa with garden. Ideal for families but far from the city center.

✚ C4 ✉ Hernalser Hauptstrasse 187 ☎ 486 6620 🚋 Tram 43 from Schottentor or Schnellbahn to Hernals

HOTEL-PENSION ARENBERG ($$)

A Best Western hotel; unpretentious and friendly.

✚ J6 ✉ Stubenring 2 ☎ 512 5291 🚋 Trams 1, 2 to Stubenring

HOTEL-PENSION MUSEUM ($$)

Art lovers and academics are attracted to this old-fashioned pension with large rooms. Close to the Kunsthistorisches Museum.

✚ G6 ✉ Museumstrasse 3 ☎ 523 5127 🚇 U3 to Volkstheater

HOTEL WANDL ($$)

Popular pension next to Peterskirche in a partly 12th-century building.

✚ H6 ✉ Petersplatz 9 ☎ 534 55-0; fax 534 55-77 🚇 U1, U3 to Stephansplatz

KUGEL ($)

Extremely good value near the lively Spittelberg neighborhood, which is full of open-air restaurants in summer.

✚ G7 ✉ Siebensterngasse 43 ☎ 523 3355; fax 523 3355-5 🕓 Closed early Jan–early Feb 🚋 Tram 49 from Dr. Karl-Renner-Ring

PENSION AM OPERNECK ($)

In this six-room bed and breakfast, they bring breakfast to your room.

✚ H6 ✉ Kärntner Strasse 47 ☎ 512 9310 🚇 U1, U2, U4 to Oper

PENSION CHRISTINA ($)

Central, and close to the trendy Bermuda Triangle area (➤ 18). The 33 rooms are small but have an unpretentious charm.

✚ H6 ✉ Hafnersteig 7 ☎ 533 2961; fax 533 2961-11 🚇 U1, U4 to Schwedenplatz

PENSION LANDHAUS FUHRGASSL-HUBER ($$)

In a wine village by the Vienna Woods. With its peasant-style furniture and a summer courtyard, this one is special.

✚ C1 ✉ Rathstrasse 24, Neustift am Walde ☎ 440 3033 🚌 Bus 35A from junction Krottenbach/Silberstrasse. Tram 38 from Schottentor

PENSION NOSSEK ($$)

Good location in the heart of the city; the pedestrianized area ensures quiet. The 26 rooms range from spacious to compact. Pleasant service. Reserve well in advance.

✚ H6 ✉ Graben 17 ☎ 533 7041; fax 535 3646 🚇 U1, U3 to Stephansplatz

PENSION PERTSCHY ($$)

Pleasant and friendly, this pension is just off the Graben. Rooms are spacious with period furniture.

✚ H6 ✉ Habsburgergasse 5 ☎ 534 49-0; fax 534 49-49 🚇 U1, U3 to Stephansplatz

VIENNA
travel facts

ARRIVING & DEPARTING

Before you go

- No visas are required for citizens of the EU and other Western European countries, or for citizens of the U.S. and Canada.
- No vaccinations are required.
- Some wooded areas of Austria are home to *Zecken*, a kind of tick whose bite can transmit encephalitis, which in a few cases proves fatal. Viennese hikers are vaccinated against it. Inquire at the Austrian consulate about precautions.

When to go

- Vienna is delightful in spring and even more so in fall.
- Most of the important arts events are held in spring and early summer. The main opera and concert seasons kick-off in fall.
- Some prime attractions (such as the Lipizzaners and the Vienna Boys Choir) take a long summer break from about July to September and may be on tour some months. Plan ahead.

Climate

- The average year-round temperature is 50°F (10°C); however, it is hot in mid-summer (often over 86°F (30°C) and very cold in December, January, and February.
- If you suffer from migraines or circulation problems you may be affected by the *Föhn* wind blowing off the Alps in winter.

Arriving by air

- Vienna International Airport is east of the city at Schwechat (12 miles) ☎ 7007 2231, 2232 or 2233; arrivals: 7007 22197; departures: 7007 22184
- Connection to downtown is by shuttle bus to the City Air Terminal/Hilton (Am Stadtpark), or to the Westbahnhof via Südbahnhof.
- City Air Terminal Bus (24-hour service) information ☎ 580 0354
- An S-Bahn (*Schnellzug*) runs hourly (5AM–10PM) between the airport and Wien Mitte/Landstrasser Hauptstrasse.
- Taxis cost around AS300–500, depending on destination.

Arriving by rail

- There are two international stations: the Westbahnhof for Western Austria and Western Europe; and the Südbahnhof for Southern and Eastern Austria, Eastern and Southern Europe, and the Czech Republic.
- Franz-Josefs-Bahnhof is for trains to Northern Austria.
- Train information ☎ 1717 (24 hours); reservations 1700

Arriving by car

- Vienna is reached from Bavaria/Salzburg via the West Autobahn (A1); from the south it is reached from Graz and the Italian border via the South Autobahn (A2); and from the Hungarian border it is reached via the East Autobahn (A4).

Arriving by bus

- International bus lines arrive at Wien Mitte/Landstrasser Hauptstrasse 1B, which is also the station for most domestic lines ☎ 712 0453 (Eurolines)

Arriving by boat

- May to September, cruise ships run on the Danube between Passau (Germany) and Vienna.
- Ships dock at the *Donaudampf schiffsgesellschaft* (DDSG) berth

near the Reichsbrücke (close to U1 Vorgartenstrasse) ☎ 217 500

Customs regulations

• Duty-free limits for non-European Union visitors are: 200 cigarettes or 250g of tobacco or 50 cigars; 2 liters of wine and 1 liter of spirits.

ESSENTIAL FACTS

Electricity

• The voltage is 220V AC and two-pin plugs are used.

Etiquette

• Titles are important; if you know which one to use (eg *Herr Doktor*), use it. Address the waiter as *Herr Ober*, the waitress as *Fräulein*.

Money matters

• On January 1, 1999 the euro became the official currency of Austria and the Austrian Schilling became a denomination of the euro. Austrian Schilling notes and coins continue to be legal tender during a transitional period. Euro bank notes are likely to start to be introduced by January 1, 2002.

• The unit of currency is the Austrian Schilling, abbreviated to ATS or AS. Currency is issued in denominations of (notes) AS20, AS50, AS100, AS500, AS1,000, and AS5,000; (coins) AS1, AS5, AS10, and AS20.

• Credit cards are accepted by most hotels, leading stores, and more expensive restaurants.

• Machines on Kärntner Strasse and Stephansplatz give Schillings for foreign banknotes.

• ATM machines giving cash

against international credit or debit cards with PIN numbers are plentiful in the center.

National holidays

• Jan 1, Jan 6 (Epiphany), Easter Monday, May 1, Christi Himmelfahrt (Ascension Day), Corpus Christi (Thu after Whitsun), Aug 15 (Assumption of the Virgin), Oct 26 (National Day), Nov 1 (All Saints), Dec 8 (Annunciation), Dec 24–26 (everything closes from midday on Christmas Eve.

Opening hours

• Stores: Mon–Fri 9–6; Sat 9–5 (food stores may open earlier). Retailers now have the option of Saturday opening, but outside the main shopping areas, many remain closed from noon onwards. Almost all stores are open 9–6 on the four Saturdays before Christmas.

• Banks: Mon–Wed, Fri 8–12:30, 1:30–3; Thu 1:30–5:30. In the center some stay open at lunch.

• Offices: Mon–Fri 8–4, but may close earlier on Friday.

Places of worship

• The Tourismus Pastoral office issues a booklet with details of services for all Christian denominations and Judaism, and where confession in foreign languages may be made ✉ Stephansplatz 6, 6th floor ☎ 5155 23530

• Anglican: Christ Church ✉ Jaurèsgasse 17–19 ☎ 714 8900

• Islamic: Islamic Centre ✉ Am Hubertusdamm 17–19, Floridsdorf ☎ 263 2120-0

• Jewish: City Synagogue ✉ Seitenstettengasse 4 ☎ 531 04103 or 104

• Vienna Community Church ✉ Reformierte Stadtkirche, Dorotheergasse 16 ☎ 505 5233

- Methodist: ✉ Sechshauser Strasse 56 ☎ 893 6989
- Roman Catholic (in English and other languages): St. Augustin ✉ 1 Augustinerstrasse ☎ 533 7099

Student travelers

- There are nine youth hostels. You need an International Youth Hostel Federation membership card, obtainable on the spot.
- Österreichischer Jugend-herbergsverband (Austrian Youth Hostel Association) ✉ Schottering 28 ☎ 533 5353
- From July 1 to September 30, student hostels in the city become *Saison Hotels*: information from Academia Hotels ✉ Pfeilgasse 3A, A-1080 ☎ 401 7620. There are simple, well-kept rooms for students at the Kolping Movement Centre: Kolpingfamilie ✉ Bendlgasse 10–noon ☎ 813 5487

Time differences

- Austria observes Central European Time, 6–9 hours ahead of U.S. time zones, 1 hour ahead of GMT.

PUBLIC TRANSPORTATION

Integrated system

- Vienna is covered in an overlapping network of *U-Bahn* (underground), *Strassenbahn* (trams) and buses.
- Maps of the transportation network can be obtained at the Opern Passage/Karlsplatz information counter of the U-Bahn ☎ 790 9105
- Newsagents (*Tabak Trafik*) sell tickets for public transportation. Main U-Bahn and S-Bahn stations have ticket counters. An easy one to find is at the Karlsplatz end of the Opern Passage, at the entrance to U1, U2, U4.
- A single ride card must be validated at the entrance to the underground, or on a tram or bus, using the stamping machines. It can be used for one unbroken ride, including changes of line, or changes from U-Bahn, to tram, to bus. Valid one hour from stamping.
- Penalties for traveling without a valid ticket are heavy and checks quite frequent.

Types of ticket

- Excursion or season tickets are valid on all parts of the network and even on suburban buses (up to the city boundary).
- Individual tickets are much more expensive per ride, and the machines dispensing them on trams are complicated.
- Good value weekly tickets allow unlimited travel all over the network for seven days. No photo is required.
- *8 Tage-Karte* (8 strips) each valid for 24 hours' travel all over the network. If there are two or more of you, validate one strip per person.
- You can buy blocks of tickets for single rides, as well as 24-hour and 72-hour time tickets (useful for weekend visitors).
- Time tickets and the *Umwelt-Streifennetzkarte* must be validated once at the commencement of the period of use and are then good for the period stipulated.

U-Bahn

- There are five lines, the newest (U3) still under construction. U2 follows a semi-circular route covering half the Ringstrasse.

- The U-Bahn maps found on platforms are color-coded and also show connections to other forms of transportation. Be careful to note the end-stop of the direction you want; this will be shown on the illuminated sign of the appropriate platform.
- Three lines (U1, U2, U4) meet at the Oper/Karlsplatz.
- Main stations have elevators and escalators.
- You may take bicycles into designated cars (except during rush hour).
- The S-Bahn (*Schnellbahn*) is a rapid transit railway bringing commuters from the suburbs to the major traffic connections of the city.

Trams/buses

- The route is clearly marked at the tram stop and on a card inside. Check you are traveling in the right direction.
- Bus routes fill the gaps between the mostly radial tram lines. Night buses on main routes run every 30 minutes from Schwedenplatz after 12:30AM until around 5AM on Fridays, Saturdays, and the night before a public holiday. A supplement is payable.
- The small hopper buses (1A, 2A and 3A) have circular routes through the Inner City with stops at or near virtually all places of interest. They run only during normal working hours.

Taxis

- Cabs are efficient and not unreasonably expensive by Austrian standards.
- You can order a cab by phone ☎ 31 300, 40 100 or 60 160. The operator will give you a time of arrival (normally between three and seven minutes).
- Tips are 10 percent.
- There are supplements for late-night or weekend rides, plus per head and per piece of luggage.

MEDIA & COMMUNICATIONS

Newspapers & magazines

- Foreign newspapers are available from newsstands in the center (open normal business hours), and from the Südbahnhof and Westbahnhof newsstands (open until 10PM).
- *Falter* (in German) is a mixture of comprehensive listings and agitprop. Its movie section includes the program of the Österreichisches Filmmuseum (▶ 83).
- The English-language *Austria Today* appears weekly on Tuesdays.

Post offices

- Post offices are open Mon–Fri 8–noon, 2–6.
- There are 24-hour post offices at:
  ✉ Fleischmarkt 19 ☎ 515 090
  ✉ Südbahnhof ☎ 501 810
  ✉ Westbahnhof ☎ 891 150
- Stamps are sold at post offices and at *Tabak Trafik* shops.

Radio & television

- Cable television is widely available.
- An English-language program, *Hello Austria, Hello Vienna*, is broadcast on Saturdays at 12:30PM on the second channel (ORF 2).
- There is news in English and in French every morning on the radio (on Österreich 1) at 8AM.

Telephones

- Telephone cards are sold in *Tabak Trafik* shops (newsstands) and at post offices. Some telephones in the Kohlmarkt/Graben area take credit cards.
- Directory assistance: Austria ☎ 118 11, Germany ☎ 118 12

EMERGENCIES

Embassies & consulates

- Australia ✉ Mattiellistrasse 2–4 ☎ 5128 5800
- Canada ✉ Laurenzerberg 2 ☎ 5313 830 00
- Ireland ✉ Hilton-Centre, 16th Floor, Landstrasser Hauptstrasse 2A ☎ 7154 2460
- New Zealand ✉ Springsiedlgasse 28 ☎ 318 8505
- U.K. ✉ Jaurésgasse 10 ☎ 7161 35151
- U.S. ✉ Boltzmangasse 16 ☎ 313 39 (embassy) or ✉ Gartenbaupromenade 2 (next to Marriott Hotel) ☎ 31 339-3005 (consulate)

Emergency phone numbers

- Ambulance ☎ 144
- Doctor on call ☎ 141
- Dentist ☎ 512 2078
- Fire ☎ 122
- Police ☎ 133
- ÖAMTC (breakdown service equivalent of AAA) ☎ 120
- Befrienders (Samaritans in Vienna) ☎ 713 3374 (English speaking)

Lost property

- Report loss or theft to the nearest police station.
- Lost Property Bureau ✉ Wasagasse 22 ☎ 313 4492-11 🕔 Mon–Fri 8–noon
- Railroad Lost Property ✉ Westbahnhof 🕔 Mon–Fri 8–3 (you must call in person); ✉ Südbahuhof ☎ 5800 35656
- Vienna Transportation System Lost Property ☎ 790 943 -500

Medical treatment

- Vienna General Hospital (Allgemeines Krankenhaus) ✉ Währinger Gürtel 18–20 ☎ 40 400-1964
- The Barmherzige Brüder (Brothers of Mercy) treat patients for free at their hospital ✉ Mohrengasse 9 (2nd District) ☎ 211 21-0

Medicines

- Pharmacies are normally open Mon–Fri 8–noon, 2–6; Sat 8–noon.
- English-speaking pharmacists: Internationale Apotheke ✉ Kärntner Ring 17 ☎ 512 2825; Schweden-Apotheke, Pharmacie Internationale, ✉ Schwedenplatz 2 ☎ 533 29110

Sensible precautions

- Lock valuables in your hotel safe and don't carry large amounts of cash. Crime is low in Vienna, but high season pickpockets are busy.
- Women can feel secure, even after dark. Avoid the main railroad stations at night and the red-light district along the Gürtel.
- The old-style gallantry with which women are treated, especially by older men, is often a figleaf for rampant male chauvinism.

Visitors with disabilities

- Facilities have improved in museums and some other sights, but older trams and buses remain impossible for anyone in a wheelchair. Many smaller U-Bahn stations still lack elevators.
- A travel agent specializing in the needs of those with disabilities is Egnatia Tours ✉ Piaristengasse 60 ☎ 406 9732-0

LANGUAGE

Days of the week
Monday Montag
Tuesday Dienstag
Wednesday Mittwoch
Thursday Donnerstag
Friday Freitag
Saturday Samstag
Sunday Sonntag

Numbers

1 eins	11 elf
2 zwei	12 zwölf
3 drei	13 dreizehn
4 vier	14 vierzehn
5 fünf	15 fünfzehn
6 sechs	16 sechszehn
7 sieben	17 siebzehn
8 acht	18 achtzehn
9 neun	19 neunzehn
10 zehn	20 zwanzig

Useful words and phrases
yes/no ja/nein
please bitte
thank you (very much) danke
(schön)
I'm sorry verzeihung
excuse me, please entschuldigen
Sie, bitte
do you speak English? sprechen
Sie englisch?
I do not understand ich verstehe
nicht
how much does that cost? wieviel
kostet das?
do you take credit cards? darf ich
mit Kreditkarte zahlen?
good night gute Nacht
good morning guten Morgen *or*
(more usually) Grüss Gott
good afternoon guten Abend
today/tomorrow heute/morgen
here/there hier, da/dort
what? was?
when/where wann/wo
right/left rechts/links
straight on geradeaus
near/far nahe, in der Nähe/weit

GLOSSARY OF ARCHITECTURAL STYLES

Romanesque
9th to 12th centuries.
Characterized by the round arch.
Parts of St. Stephen's and the
Ruprechtskirche are almost the
only surviving examples in
Vienna.

Gothic
Early 14th to mid-16th centuries.
Features include pointed arches
and rib vaulting, exemplified by
the main part of St. Stephen's.

Renaissance
From about 1530. The Stallburg,
Schweizertor, and Amalienburg of
the Hofburg are among the few
Viennese examples.

Baroque
1620–1780. Very theatrical and
ornate, baroque came to Vienna
from Italy during the Counter-
Reformation. Late baroque
merges into the playful style of
rococo.

Classicism
1770s–1840s. Plain and dignified.
The leading exponent in Vienna
was Joseph Kornhäusel.

Historicism
1858–1918. The buildings
flanking the Ringstrasse are
examples of this style reproducing
the architecture of earlier epochs,
but with its own flair.

Secession
1897–1918. Known as art nouveau
in France and Jugendstil in
German-speaking countries. A
sensual style with flowing lines
and often using gilding and
vegetation as ornament.

93

INDEX

Citypack
Vienna

AUTHOR *Louis James*
MANAGING EDITOR *Jackie Staddon*
COVER DESIGN *Tigist Getachew*
COVER PICTURES *AA Picture Library*

Copyright	©Automobile Association Developments Limited 1996, 2001
Maps copyright	©Automobile Association Developments Limited 1996, 2001
Fold-out map:	© RV Reise-und Verkehrsvenag Munich · Stuttgart
	© Cartography: GeoData

Fodor's is a registered trademark of Random House, Inc.
Published in the United Kingdom by AA Publishing

ISBN 0-676-90158-1
Second Edition

Acknowledgments
The Automobile Association wishes to thank the following photographers, libraries, and assocations for their assistance in the preparation of this book: Austrain National Tourist Office 6, 12, 19, 21, 25b, 36, 46b; Allsport/MSI 9. All remaining pictures are held in the Association's own library (AA Photo Library) and were taken by C Sawyer with the exception of the following: pages 13b, 87a, which were taken by M Adleman; pages 1, 31, 37, 38a, 40, 43b, 44b, 46a, 60, 87b, which were taken by D Noble; and pages 5a, 5b, 7, 13a, 23, 27, 29, 39b, 44a, 48a, 49a, 50, 54, 55, 56b, 59a, 59b, 61, which were taken by M Siebert.

Important tip
Time inevitably brings changes, so always confirm prices, travel facts, and other perishable information when it matters. Although Fodor's cannot accept responsiblity for errors, you can use this guide in the confidence that we have taken every car to ensure its accuracy.

Special sales
Fodor's Travel Publications are available at special discounts for bulk purchases (100 copies or more) for sales promotions or premiums. Special editions, including personalized covers, excerpts of existing guides, and corporate imprints, can be created in large quantities for special needs. For more information, contact your local bookseller or write to Special Markets, Fodor's Travel Publications, 280 Park Avenue, New York, NY 10017. Inquiries from Canada should be directed to your local Canadian bookseller or sent to Random House of Canada, Ltd., Marketing Department, 2775 Matheson Blvd. East, Mississauga, Ontario L4W 4P7.

Color separation by Daylight Colour Art Pte Ltd, Singapore
Manufactured by Dai Nippon Printing Co. (Hong Kong) Ltd
10 9 8 7 6 5 4 3 2 1

Titles in the Citypack series
- Amsterdam • Barcelona • Beijing • Berlin • Boston • Brussels & Bruges •
- Chicago • Dublin• Florence • Hong Kong • Lisbon • London • Los Angeles •
- Madrid • Melbourne • Miami • Montreal • Munich • New York • Paris •
- Prague • Rome • San Francisco • Seattle • Shanghai • Singapore • Sydney •
- Tokyo • Toronto • Venice • Vienna • Washington, D.C. •